YOUTH FOOTBALL

A NEW COACH'S GUIDE TO GOOD DECISION-
MAKING, BUILDING A WINNING TEAM, AND
DEVELOPING YOUNG ATHLETES

C.R. EDWARDS

CONTENTS

INTRODUCTION

Have you played football as a child or in high school and want to give back to the community by mentoring children? Have you coached little league basketball, soccer, or baseball but want to coach youth football? Or do you have minimal experience as a youth football assistant coach and wish to become a head coach?

If you've answered any of the above questions with a "yes," then Youth Football: A New Coach's Guide to Good Decision-Making, Building a Winning Team, and Developing Young Athletes is for you.

Children who participate in physical activity, such as playing football, perform better academically than those who don't. Additionally, they experience better overall health. Most importantly, such children are less likely to suffer from diseases such as childhood obesity and diabetes (Project Play, n.d.). You can make a difference in children's lives and help them become better adults. You may produce the next Tom Brady, Patrick Mahomes, or Derick Henry.

When building a youth football team, you'll likely face challenges. Aren't challenges opportunities to grow? Some of the challenges will include:

- Dealing with negative or uninvested parents
- Having quality assistant coaches
- Proper planning on how to run an efficient, safe, and fun practice
- This is where this book will serve as a great tool. By the time you finish reading it, you should:
- Have the competence and confidence to build a successful youth football program
- Own a system that will ensure a child's success on the football field and in life
- Learn how to troubleshoot or avoid common mistakes that new football coaches make

I've structured this book so that you can get the maximum impact from it. It introduces you to the qualities you need to become an elite youth football coach. For example, no elite coach disregards the safety of their players, which is why they begin by teaching children the fundamentals of football. In Chapter 1, you'll learn ten qualities you should have to develop great players and great people.

One of the challenges new youth football coaches face is dealing with uninterested parents. The thing is that parents can only be interested if they're involved. In Chapter 2, you'll discover how to include parents in your preparation for the upcoming season. You'll also learn to find quality assistant coaches, a critical part of your staff.

Chapter 3 shifts attention to the football field. Assuming that your assistant coaches, parents, and players know youth football rules is a mistake. How would you plan your practices and games? This chapter explains why you need to know your league's rules. Additionally, it introduces you to the fundamentals of the game of football, how to teach the three-point stance, and how to ensure the safety of your players.

Nothing is as powerful as planning when coaching youth football. This is the subject. Chapter 4 focuses on but purely regarding planning practices. It's rare for a football player to execute a play they have yet to practice successfully. You also can't expect to play a formation players see for the first time in a game; it won't work. That's why you and your team need to practice.

To be effective, your practices must be in black and white. You'll learn why in this chapter.

In Chapter 5, it's time to drill your players into the techniques to win games. Those drills are classified according to the phases of football: offense, defense, and special teams. For each phase, you'll learn ten drills that teach your players skills and techniques that make them effective. For example, you'll discover a drill that ensures an error-free exchange between the quarterback and the ball carrier.

Once you've learned about the 30 drills in Chapter 5, you'll then focus on how to coach offense. In Chapter 6, you'll discover what to consider when designing your offense, the strategy for offensive play calling, and the importance of scouting your opponent's defense. This chapter also covers eight offensive formations you can instill and implement. When you're done with this chapter, you should know which formation suits you and your time.

Chapter 7 teaches you how to defend effectively. You'll begin by learning the fundamentals of successful defense, such as stance, alignment, and covering the receiver. The defensive line is key to your defense, which is why this chapter shows you how best to shed blocks, anchor gaps, and squeeze. The last part of this chapter deals with six top defense schemes for youth football.

In Chapter 8, you learn about how to coach special teams. Your special teams can differentiate between a win and a loss, especially if the game is close. All players in your special teams, such as the kicker, holder, punter, long snapper, and short snapper, must know how to execute their roles. This chapter will guide you on how to coach each of these players. Additionally, you learn how your team can ensure they score and prevent conceding extra points.

There comes a time when your youth football team will have to play the first game. Preparations and the time for execution for you and your team would be complete. You should know what you can and can't do when coaching during the game. Of course, the game starts at practice and includes what players should eat. The key during the game is what you and your coaches do, which you'll learn in Chapter 9.

In Chapter 10, you'll learn what the end of the season means and what you should consider doing. For example, whether you've won the league or ended last, the team, you, and individual players have reason to celebrate. Why not honor all those who made it possible to participate in youth football during the previous season? This chapter will guide you on what you should do at the end of the season.

I know I've made big promises about what this book can do for you. Naturally, you'll be skeptical because you've probably never heard about me. You may be wondering what qualifies me to write such a book. Wonder no more because here's what you should know about me and my credentials in football.

It's no understatement that I love football. I played football from the age of eight until I turned 18. During my playing days, I've learned what separates high-quality coaching from poor coaching. I've worked with coaches who rarely had practice and game plans. Inevitably, such coaches lost more games than they count. In contrast, coaches who took time to work on the fundamentals, plan for practices and games, and focus on developing the whole person, produced much better results.

Not only do I love football, but I also have a heart for youth development and service through sports, specifically football. It should be no surprise that I've served as a volunteer football coach for two years. This allowed me to implement many ideas I've included in this book. Over the years, I've learned and understand what it takes to cultivate a culture of winning both on the field and in life.

Coaching youth football can be challenging and has a steep learning curve. I desire to help you reduce this learning curve and become confident to start and sustain a successful youth football program. This matters deeply to me because I'll be contributing toward developing coaches who'll become part of a select group of wildly successful youth football coaches.

If what I offer sounds good, let's start reading and applying the ideas in this book!

1

TEN QUALITIES OF AN ELITE YOUTH COACH

W inning on the football field is excellent, but it can feel unfulfilling if there are severe issues in the players' lives beyond the game. Waiting until players are older before teaching them life and football skills is often too late. The coach is crucial in embedding these positive life skills while children are still young. Most importantly, children learn by copying from others around them. This is why a newbie football coach must have the good qualities of football and life. This chapter focuses on ten essential qualities that every elite coach possesses.

THEY FOCUS ON THE FUNDAMENTALS AND SAFETY OF PLAYERS

It's easy to assume that your assistant coaches and youth players know the rules and fundamentals of football. Thinking so might be a recipe for misunderstanding and failure to develop the talents of both your coaching staff and players. To ensure you both are on the same page, it's worth beginning the season by reviewing football's core fundamentals and rules. It's a good idea to re-read your youth football league's rules. We'll get to the fundamentals of football shortly.

ELITE COACHES TEACH INTEGRITY

Parents and coaches often discuss the importance of working hard, winning, giving 120%, or becoming top players. What many of these parents and coaches tend to exclude from their conversations is the value of players becoming people of integrity. A person and football player with integrity is honest, trustworthy, a great friend, and reliable to teammates and the community.

What does the term integrity mean? The word originates from the Latin word integritatem, which means "soundness, wholeness, or completeness" (Online Etymology Dictionary, 2021). John Wooden, the famed

American basketball coach, and player, defined integrity as follows:

> Integrity, in its simplest form, is the purity of intention. It's keeping a clean conscience. But it is also a composite of some of the other mortar qualities in the pyramid. Integrity contains a bit of reliability, a healthy helping of honesty, and a portion of sincerity. However, the component of purity of intention is important enough to give integrity the status of mortar in its own right. (Implement, 2017)

Teammates, fans, and coaches can depend upon a football player with integrity—what better time to develop this highly sought-after quality than when they're young? Otherwise, the older they become and the further they advance their football careers, the worse they may become. When someone exhibits integrity, they're blameless and stay true no matter the situation.

Integrity, like nearly all human behaviors, is learned, not necessarily an inherent quality. This means that the best method of teaching integrity to your football players is to be a person of integrity. Teach your players to keep promises. Saying one thing and doing the opposite isn't a sign of having integrity. Two opportunities will arise to educate your players to keep promises: as soon as one of them holds a promise and when one of them violates the promise they make. You could reward the player who keeps their promise to reinforce it. When you do this, do so publicly.

If your player keeps their promise, talk with them privately. Give them examples of top football players whose careers nosedived due to a lack of integrity.

Best of all, it would be best if you kept promises. In that way, you become a model for teaching integrity to your players.

ELITE COACHES ARE MASTERS OF ORGANIZATION

Adequate planning is crucial to having a successful season when coaching youth football. We'll discuss this subject in more detail in the next chapter that deals with preparation.

The elements of successful youth coaching that constitute an organized elite coach include planning practices, planning parent meetings, establishing proper coaches, and preparing early parent meetings. We'll get deeper into each of these elements in Chapter 2.

THEY KEEP EVERY PRACTICE UPBEAT

Practice is a time to teach most of the skills you want your players to learn. You can teach those skills like a solemn Navy SEAL or a no-nonsense schoolmaster. I understand that seriousness is necessary, but it should be a minor theme in your coaching career. However, many young players will soon stop coming to practice or be uninterested if they show up.

Children learn better in a playful and fun environment. They learn faster when serious work is turned into fun and social activities. That's why you must keep practice exciting and fun. Make it a big deal when a player makes a huge play. How do you keep your players interested and excited to play for you? There are three ways to achieve this.

Coach with excitement and enthusiasm: Children, like most people, respond positively to excitement and enthusiasm. Your demeanor influences the attitude of your players. If you get hyped up when a player makes a good play, it'll rub off on the other players. In contrast, if you act negatively and are constantly boring, players will think you don't care. As a result, they won't care. When coaching your players at practice or on game day, choose to be in the right mind frame. All the coaching staff should look like they want to be there.

Have structured practice sessions: Most coaching time is spent on the practice field. Players quickly lose interest unless practice sessions are organized and all coaching staff understands their roles. It can be hard to regain the interest of players, and that of parents once lost. That's why it's crucial to have scripted practices and clearly defined responsibility for each coaching staff member. This will inject excitement into practices and leave positive impressions on parents and players. We'll revisit the subject of organization later.

Make practices fun: Children like having fun. Give them boring things to do; they switch off. Make practice as fun as you can, especially in the beginning. You should have intense practice sessions but blend them with fun activities once or twice every week. Try to make drills and plays as fun as possible. Your players will look forward to practice when they know it will be exciting and fun. Most importantly, ensure that the fun activities teach essential football or life skills.

ELITE COACHES COMMUNICATE WITH PARENTS EFFECTIVELY

There's no communication until a message moves from one person to the next. Misunderstanding can only be the natural outcome of failed communication. In youth football, one crucial conversation is with your players' parents during the preseason.

This meeting, called the parents' meeting, should be held before your first practice. It's a platform you use to communicate your expectations and rules with your parents. For example, you clarify your position about absences and the type of players who'll get playtime. Most importantly, you discuss with parents what you expect from them and the players and what they can look forward to when working with you and your coaching staff. Since parents' behavior can rub off on their children, you explain how you want them to behave at football games and practices. For example, you may inform your parents that they don't have to coach their son on the sidelines because it may disrupt your team's plan for the day.

There are more ideas to share about parents' communication and communication in general. Since this subject of communication is a big topic, I'll discuss it further in the next chapter.

ELITE COACHES CREATE AND MAINTAIN A HEALTHY COMPETITION AMONG PLAYERS

Football is not only about winning, but it also provides growth and mastery opportunities. Children who begin playing football must gain the basic skills to play successfully. Among them, there'll be players who progress faster than others. Naturally, there will be competition for places, which is essential for player growth. Only some of your players will accept that some children are better than them. This may create poor camaraderie among players, which is bad for creating and building a winning team and great players. Some players may quit the game or avoid competition at all costs, which denies them growth opportunities.

The antidote is to create healthy competition among your players. This is where cultivating a growth mindset will be helpful. Thinking this way enables your young players to realize that competition is necessary for growth so that they can embrace it. Benefits stemming from a type of mindset can enhance confidence, collaborative skills, and empathy—skills crucial in life and all types of sports. You can develop a healthy competitive mindset by employing the following three approaches:

- Teach children to learn from competitors: Whether it's teammates or competing team members, there are reasons players perform well. Make your players aware that competitors do well because they work harder and apply themselves more. Most importantly, let them compare their performances with their own goals, not others. The only reason to be concerned about the competition should be to learn from them.

- Explain to your players that winning results from effort: Observe how your players exert themselves in practice and games. Link the results they achieve with their efforts to illustrate that winning is the outcome of effort. You'll need to repeat this often, so it sticks in your players' minds.

- Develop a healthy team culture: Teach your players the value of reflecting on their performance in practice and at games. The aim is to get them to learn what they did well and what they can improve. This shifts the focus from competitors to themselves. Moreover, it helps develop a growth mindset.

THEY TEACH RESILIENCE AMID TOUGH SITUATIONS

Do you consider yourself resilient? When things don't go your way, do you stay down or stand up and go at it again? Setbacks will surely hit you and your young football players. How would you like them to react to those setbacks and challenges? Surely you want them to have resilience, especially if you want them to showcase their football skills at the top levels in the future.

The test of your resilience comes when your players face setbacks. For example, suppose your team concedes an interception that opponents turn into a touchdown. Such a time calls for calmness, but often, coaches yell and scream at the player who makes a mistake. Imagine how such a reaction could impact young players such as yours! Reminding them of their mistake doesn't make them a better player but a timid one. A nervous player won't take calculated risks during practice or in the game.

How do you develop resilience while helping your players cultivate it? The best place to foster resilience is on the practice field. For example, have the children perform certain plays while exhausted. In this type of condition, many of them will make mistakes such as dropping the ball. Go to the player who dropped the ball and throw it to them until they catch it.

Another technique for developing resilience in your players is to practice situational football. For example, you can have them practice hurrying up offense or goal line defense. These tense situations will prepare your team to deal with challenges. Drill these practices numerous times so that they know how to deal with them during a game.

ELITE COACHES REWARD HARD WORK

Imagine this situation: A young back scores a first-quarter touchdown and, with arms raised, jogs off the field thinking, "Look at me. I've arrived." The crowd cheers the young player more than they celebrate many school graduations. Celebrating significant results such as scoring touchdowns is wonderful, but it brings societal and sporting challenges.

- It can breed unsupportive teammates: If we only recognize results, what incentivizes teammates to support and help the players who score touchdowns and extra points? I bet there's none.
- Develops players who lack integrity: A player who's incentivized to achieve results will do nearly anything to produce those results. Instead of thinking about the team, they focus on themselves. They have a scarcity mindset, preventing the team from winning and teammates from becoming great people and players.
- No improvement: A player recognized for results tends to believe they're the best, which is fine. However, many players stop stretching their comfort zones and taking on new

challenges. As a result, their performance stays the same and often results in negative team results.

The solution is to reward your players for their effort, whether in games, practice, or life in general. Look everywhere in life and you'll notice that results always come from effort, especially for players who don't possess natural talents. For example, reward a player who consistently shows up in the gym to build their upper body and calf muscle strengths.

Something is amazing about focusing on effort. It's that effort can be controlled, meaning it can be improved while results can't. All results indicate how well your players apply themselves on the football field. Recognizing effort makes players think as teammates—not as individuals—improving the team's culture and results. Rewarding effort also enables you to recognize players that make teammates better.

ELITE COACHES VALUE AND TEACH DISCIPLINE

What does discipline mean to you? Most people associate the word discipline with punishment. After all, that's what places like school and home teach us from childhood. Many of us recall images of our parents yelling at us to change our behaviors when we hear the word discipline. Although punishment is part of discipline, more is needed to give a complete and accurate picture of this human quality.

There's no doubt that discipline is a central tenet in every athlete's success, both on and off the field. I like to define discipline, or better, self-discipline, as giving myself a command and following it. This definition puts the onus on each player to do what they tell themselves they will do. In sports, business, or relationships, discipline will help you succeed.

Based on the above definition of discipline, you must include responsibility and self-control. American jails are full of inmates because they lack self-control and act irrationally. The same can happen on the football field, which is why helping your young players to cultivate self-discipline is one of the most important jobs of a youth football coach.

How do you help your players to develop discipline, responsibility, and self-control? Here are important ways you can implement them:

- Set expectations early and get all players and parents to commit. This is crucial because once all the stakeholders commit, the expectations become theirs, not just yours. Furthermore, consider including repercussions for going against those expectations. Just as important—perhaps more important—be the first to follow those expectations.

- Confront discipline issues early. As soon as you spot discipline problems, implement corrective measures as early as possible. This sets the precedent that indiscipline can't be tolerated and prevents things from worsening.

- Understand the personalities of all your players. Addressing the entire group rather than individuals can breed negativity, which is a bad attitude and is unwanted in a football team. If you have to criticize a player, do so privately rather than publicly. Dealing with an individual allows you to direct disciplinary actions effectively with minimal side effects.

- Apply unusual corrective behaviors. For example, you can give a sharp command or be silent in the right circumstances to show disapproval. This approach is practical when used sparingly.

Various approaches to dealing with discipline allow a youth coach to choose the right one for each player and circumstance.

ELITE COACHES HAVE DEPENDABLE FOOTBALL SYSTEMS

No matter how talented your young players might be, they will only develop into great players if they play a football system that suits their skill sets. For this to happen, you and your coaching staff must understand your chosen football system. It's imperative to select a youth football special team, defense, and offense system that draws the best from your players.

Whatever football system you select, make sure it provides a balance between offense and defense. Also, the system should offer balance on offense or defense. For example, your team needs to attack outside, off-tackle, and inside. On defense, have a system that blends aggressive blitzes and safe looks that give the minimal opposition opportunity for big plays. Including deception in your football system can confuse the opposition, allowing your team to make huge plays.

2

HOW TO PREPARE FOR THE SEASON

B efore any player sets foot on the football field's grass for the new season, the whole team must be prepared to compete. These preparations are the base of a strong and winning team establishment. Successful preparations require planning, well-vetted head and assistant coaches, invested parents, and determined players. As a coach, you need to be prepared to prepare your team, and this chapter guides those preparations. You'll learn everything about season planning, including scouting and staff development. Are you ready to build a successful team for the next season? Let's get started.

SEASON PLANNING

What do you want to achieve with your team this coming season? What are your goals, and how are you going to achieve them? The answer to those questions lies in season planning. A season plan is the only effective way of mapping out all your team goals, scouting and finding talent, building a solid technical staff, and planning for weekly and daily practice.

There are three phases around which you can plan and prepare for your next season: preseason, season, and postseason. Let's look at each one of these phases in more detail.

Preseason: A preseason is when the team and coaches participate in a series of scrimmage games for training. This is part of season preparations, where coaches can organize their teams. Preseason offers youth football coaches like you opportunities to scout talents, build their teams' technical staff, and develop their football systems.

Regular season: This is the period when your team plays official league games. The skills gained during the preseason period are put into action. In this period, every game carries weight—there are points at stake. The competition is on. In this phase, you are faced with the following tasks:

- Team playing style
- Practice plan—we will discuss this in more detail in the following chapter
- Defensive installation that proved to be effective
- Offensive play installation that proved to work during the preseason

Postseason: Following the regular season comes the postseason phase.

During the postseason, teams will participate in playoff games. After one or two playoff games (based on league regulations), two teams will compete in the championship game. The championship winner will be crowned the champion of that respective league. Following the pos

- The end-of-season activities involve:
- Team banquet
- Coach Appreciation
- Parents' appreciation
- A survey of parents' satisfaction with the team's performances
- Fan satisfaction survey

Football is a technical game and requires thorough technical planning. You must create a program that effectively conducts weekly and daily practice properly. As mentioned, it takes more than just a coach to build a strong team—you need strong players, parents, and assistant coaches to build a winning team.

You may have heard the adage, "Proper planning prevents poor performance." If there's one place where it is of great significance, it's in youth football.

FINDING QUALITY ASSISTANT COACHES

To build a strong quality team, you must have passionate and skilled assistants and head coaches. Each assistant coach needs to accommodate and interact healthily with every player, be able to sort out the strengths and weaknesses of each player, and be professional. Quality assistant coaches must be reachable to all the children. The roles and responsibilities of an assistant coach include:

- Overseeing all the team's activities
- Planning practices and preparing for games
- Maintaining training equipment and facility
- Evaluating team performance
- Motivating and instilling the importance of team unity
- Supervising training sessions
- Maintaining and keeping games records

How do you find the right assistant coach for your youth football team? Selecting an assistant coach always begins with gathering more information about the potential candidate. This requires asking candidates the right questions. Here are some of the questions I've found to be helpful to ask potential assistant coaches:

- Have you coached, or do you coach relatives? This question may reveal that the potential assistant coach has relatives within your team. If they have relatives, it's okay, but you want to know how they will handle coaching their children or other relatives. You want an assistant coach who plays no favorites when instilling discipline and teaching football skills to your youth football team. All players must receive the same treatment.

- What is your experience as a youth football coach? This question reveals the candidate's years of youth football coaching experience. You should want an assistant coach with experience, but candidates without experience are welcome. Ideally, an assistant coach should be experienced and have a positive attitude. This question can reveal only a coach's experiences but not their attitude, but it's still important.

- How do you deal with ill-mannered players? Coaching youth football is tough. Toughness and kindness are both necessary when handling disciplinary issues. Children will want to test coaches by doing unwanted things. For example, they may come late to practice to see how you'll deal with them. This question aims to find out how you'll address such players.

- What roles do you see yourself occupying come the next practice? You want assistant coaches who can plan, prepare, and supervise a practice session or game. The answer to this question will help you determine if a candidate has these skills.

What to Look for When Hiring an Assistant Coach

Getting it right can be rewarding. In any industry, the hardest part is appointing someone to fill a particular role in your team. Selecting the right assistant coach for your football team will free your time and stress and help you and the team become effective.

On the other hand, if you recruit the wrong person to your team—a person with no football chemistry and who doesn't share your football philosophy—your team will struggle to nail its season goals. Since an assistant coach can make or break your team, let's look at what qualities to look for in each candidate.

Find Someone with Loads of Respect

Find someone who respects people because they'll likely respect you as the head coach. A good assistant coach will respect your coaching philosophy and support your program. Assistant coaches who lack respect will probably rub off their bad behavior on your young players. An assistant coach who respects ordinary people will respect you, your coaching philosophy, and your coaching principles.

A Great Assistant Coach Is Loyal

Another quality that makes a great assistant coach is loyalty. You want someone you can trust with your youth football team and the staff because they'll handle your meetings and lead your team when you are absent. Hiring someone untrustworthy will destroy your team's spirit and unity.

Likely Places to Find Great Assistant Coaches

Many head coaches begin the search for assistant coaches elsewhere, forgetting to consider qualified parents, uncles, and aunts. Parents and relatives of your players are the right coaches considering they desire to see your team succeed.

Look around and identify that parent who is always available and engages well with the team—a parent whose children are comfortable and can communicate with them easily. If a parent tells you they want to help you build a winning team, why not give them that chance? They may turn out to be good assistant coaches. Of course, you still need to vet them to ensure they have the qualities you seek.

Another place you might find great coaches is scouting at other sporting events such as soccer, T-ball, or baseball. Befriend coaches who seem to be a fit within your football community and take one or three people to lunch to get to know them better. Talk with them about the youth football and hear what they have to say about it. Doing so will help you determine how knowledgeable and interested they are in youth football.

Be careful to hire an assistant coach who desires to help children and potentially wants to coach at high school or higher levels. Another source of assistant coaches is your former high school or college teammates. If you've participated in sporting events, recruit friends with whom you've forged excellent working relationships.

How Many Assistant Coaches Do You Need?

The coaching staff is responsible for bringing the best out of your youth football team through well-organized training sessions. Football is a tactical sport; coaches are responsible for designing the tactics, including formations, during games. Many drills need more than just two coaches to run. It is advisable to have a staff of more than three coaches, preferably five. One coach could handle the special teams, two coaches are enough to work with defense, and two more to focus on offense.

Having a coaching staff of at least five allows you time to think about tactics and player positions that suit your football system. You also have time to study your team's weaknesses and find ways to correct them. Since finding the right assistant coaches can take time, I recommend choosing coaches a year or two before they can start coaching your team.

Once you've found potential candidates for your assistant coach roles, you still have one more step to take. Conduct background checks on each assistant coach before bringing them to your coaching staff. A background check will reveal if someone has a criminal record or is on the run. Each one of the prospective assistant coaches must pass the background check before you can hire them. Don't even consider hiring anyone with a criminal record unless they have a long record of being clean. You don't want someone who'll make children and staff uncomfortable.

When assembling your coaching staff, remember there's a hierarchy within the team. You're the head coach, and all assistant coaches report to you. This doesn't mean you have to force instructions on them, but you work with them collaboratively. Your coaching staff should have a structure, meaning it should be clear who coordinates the defense, offense, or special teams. For this to work, establish standards and boundaries early on. All members of your coaching staff must respect the agreed-upon guidelines but allow them to exercise their authority.

If you have relatives on the coaching staff, ensure they understand your role and theirs. Nepotism doesn't work when building a successful youth football team.

BUILDING A PARENT-COACH RELATIONSHIP

Now you have the right or desired number of potential assistant coaches and a few volunteering parents. It is time you build a strong relationship with your players' parents. This is a way to have them recruit more children to come and play for your team. The truth is that every parent wants to see their child being a regular starter and shining in every game. This task is complex, especially when the child of one of the appointed assistant coaches is not a regular starter.

Seeing kids playing good football, having fun, and winning games are always exciting. Those are the rewards of coaching the youth football team. However, the exciting rewards of coaching youth football come with challenges, such as losses, setbacks, and failure.

Some parents cannot let go of bad calls by the referee. So, to avoid chaos, you need to know how to handle your parents' behavior. You might not completely control their behavior, but you can set standards early and avoid scenes witnessed when a 43-year-old youth coach was shot to death during a youth football game. This death resulted from disagreements between two football teams over a referee's decision when the Dragon Elite Academy played North Dallas United. Unfortunately, children as young as nine years witnessed the shooting and death of a youth football coach.

How to Handle Your Players' Parents

You've assembled a team of assistant coaches ready to work with the children. But before you do, one area often neglected is the parents of youth football players. Parents influence the behavior of children greatly. Bringing them closer to your team can mean a successful season as you'll minimize issues during games.

Some parents are also challenging to work with, making it necessary to have strategies to handle them. Fortunately, there's a proven approach to ensure all your players' parents behave as expected. Also, this process allows you to build healthy relationships with these parents. The process consists of two elements: conducting a preseason parent meeting and getting parents to sign a code of conduct.

Conduct a Preseason Parent Meeting

The upcoming youth football season is approaching, and a lot is expected from you and your team. Besides preparing your players for the season, you must set the stage for a smooth-running season with your players' parents. To prevent any misunderstandings and chaos during the season, you need to lay down all rules and regulations, including what's required of them, what mustn't be done, and what will happen during the season.

A preseason parent meeting is a great platform to set your expectations for the upcoming season. Here's what to cover in this first meeting with parents:

- **Introduction:** Set the stage for the meeting by clearly telling the parents who you are, your background in football coaching, and any other experience in the sport. Please explain why you're meeting with them and its importance to the team's performance.

- **Coaching philosophy:** The next item is sharing your youth football coaching philosophy. This should include how you plan to develop player skills, add fun to practices, what football system you'll use, develop players' mindsets, and instill a winning mentality.

- **Set clear expectations:** Parents need to know what you expect from players so that they can provide the necessary support. Let parents know what behavior you expect from each player to become a regular starter. Also, tell parents what kind of behavior you won't tolerate! Remember to let parents know what they can expect from you.

- **Discuss your authority:** As the head coach, parents should understand that their children are under your leadership and authority. Parents should know they have the qualities necessary to build a winning team and develop their children into great people. As a result, they should give you space to exercise your authority. Part of your role is to prepare parents for disappointments, especially while building the team. Get them to accept that some results won't be favorable, and they should learn to accept defeat.

- **Ask for volunteering fundraisers:** Youth football requires funds for teams to achieve certain goals. Specify what you'd need funds for before asking for volunteers to raise those funds. Some parents might be good at fundraising, and this meeting is ideal for asking for people who volunteer to raise funds for the team. An excellent way to find volunteers is to circulate a sign-up sheet for potential fundraisers to write their contact details. Bringing in parents this way will illustrate how keen you are as a coach to develop their children. Spell out the procedure to handle injuries: Football is a contact sport, and you can expect a few injuries. What happens when a player gets injured? Lay down the procedures to follow when a player gets injured. If you have a first-aid team to attend to players, share that information with parents. Also, inform them what you'll do to help players recover from injuries. It's essential to spell out who will take care of injured players.

- **Talk about discipline:** An undisciplined player is unlikely to become a great player and a wonderful person. Football can be an avenue to teach youth discipline. Let parents know how you're going to instill discipline within your team. Some parents might suggest ways that have worked for them at home and offer to assist with disciplinary issues.

- **Give them schedules for practice sessions and games:** Many parents strongly support their children's sporting careers. They bring their children to practices and attend practice sessions and games. They'll need schedules for practice sessions and games to plan when they'll be available to come and support the team. It will help them plan and adjust their activities and create time to be there. Moreover, they may want to know how you will travel to play away games. Give them a traveling plan.

- **Give them football rules:** Some parents love football, while some want to be there for their children without football knowledge. Parents who have yet to learn about youth football may not know how a team earns points, football positions, football terminology, and your football leagues' rules and regulations. To be on the same page with all stakeholders, hand each parent a document that outlines the rules, regulations, positions, and football terminology. This will help when you communicate with parents, players, and coaching staff.

- **Provide parents with a meeting summary:** Have someone take minutes of your meeting with parents. When the session ends, summarize what you've covered and have each parent and staff member sign the meeting minutes. This will be helpful later when dealing with unwelcome behaviors.

- **Provide every attendee with your contact details:** A parent, player, or staff member might want to contact you to discuss important matters. Provide your contact details and the times you're available to take calls. You might not be available to take their calls all the time, but you can still be accessible at certain hours.

A Parents' Code of Conduct

A code of conduct is a document that outlines expected behavior. In this case, it spells out the behaviors you expect your players' parents to showcase in practices, during the team's travels, and at games. A parents' code of conduct is essential to draw boundaries between acceptable and unacceptable behaviors. It's a must-have document to ensure parents are disciplined, especially in front of their children. A parents' code of conduct should tell parents:

- That they must respect referees' decisions and never yell at the referee
- To not punish or yell at their children during practices and games
- To be examples for their children
- Provide the coaches with space to do their work. If they have an idea that the coach can use, they should consult with the coach privately at the end of the game.
- Remember that the team is for children who should be given space to develop their football skills.
- Children will be disciplined according to guidelines, not by yelling at them.

You can include many more expected behaviors in your parents' code of conduct depending on your coaching philosophy. A tight code of conduct will protect your brand and let you do your work as a head coach. Ask each parent to sign the code of conduct to accept it.

3

THE FUNDAMENTALS OF FOOTBALL

One of the mistakes that youth football coaches make is to assume that their staff and players know their game. They erroneously undermine the teaching of football fundamentals—the basis of success. David Maraniss, the author of When Pride Still Mattered: A Life of Vince Lombardi, had this to say about Vince Lombardi regarding fundamentals:

He took nothing for granted. He began a tradition of starting from scratch, assuming that the players were blank slates who carried over no knowledge from the year before... He started with the most introductory statement of all. "Gentlemen," he said, holding a pigskin in his right hand, "this is a football." (Clear, n.d.)

It's a necessity to teach your players the fundamentals, including your league's rules. Never underestimate the importance of teaching football rules, which sets them up for success. To kick off your youth football coaching career right, let's look at what you should teach your staff and players.

LEARN YOUR LEAGUE RULES

The first and foremost thing to do before you can plan for practice is to get familiar with your league rules. Every league has rules, making it essential to check what they are and read them repeatedly to your team. Some of the regulations are explicitly directed to players, and some to the coaches. These league rules may be tweaked or updated, so to stay on their right side, review them regularly to avoid breaking them and getting penalized.

For example, a league may require that you only must have players between 5 and 10 years of age. If you need to familiarize yourself with this rule, you may play with 11-year-old children. That's the fastest way to get your team disciplined or have points forfeited. You are going to be reprimanded for such an act. They don't care whether you knew the rule or not—you broke it and will face the consequences.

Find your football league's manual and read and interpret it for your team. You can get these from your football league's website if they have one. Remember, knowing the rules ensures that your team plays its game safely.

THE FUNDAMENTALS OF FOOTBALL YOU HAVE TO KNOW

It would be best if you understand the fundamentals of knowing the game. Some of your youth players may be starters and need to know how to play football. Your primary function when coaching youth football is to teach the game. Not only are you building your brand, but you're also building someone's dream and tomorrow's football superstars. I've listed some of football's fundamentals in Chapter 1, including tackling, blocking, position names, catching, and defense concepts. We're now going to build on this knowledge.

Football Positions and Roles

The game of football, like basketball, hockey, and soccer, features a set number of positions. Those positions serve specific roles, which helps to assign tasks to every player on the field. Football positions also indicate individual lines of play, where they should be before the game kicks off.

A football game consists of three phases: offense, defense, and special teams. We'll now look at players' roles during each game phase.

Phase 1: The Offense Concept

The offense aims to score by putting the ball in the opponent's endzone. Eleven players make up the offensive unit. The offense is composed of the following positions:

Quarterback (QB): The quarterback is considered the general in the field. This player is the team leader who handles the offense. They initiate attacks, are good ball passers, and touch the ball more often than any player on their team. A QB has more options when in possession of the ball: They can pass it to the running back or run with it. Great QBs know the rules of the game and have outstanding communication skills.

Running Back (RB): The running back is a player in the offense who initiates running plays. They catch the ball from the QB, run, or pass the ball from time to time. The supreme quality of an RB is speed. There are three types of running backs:

Halfback (HB): The halfback is an RB with plenty of speed and is positioned just near the QB but behind the fullbacks. In comparison with the fullbacks, HBs are short and quick.

Fullback (FB): The fullback is an RB who protects the HB during running plays. They're bigger compared to the halfbacks. For this reason, they're often used as blockers.

Tailback (TB): A running back that focuses on running plays as the ball carrier. The TB positions just behind the QB on offense. They usually receive the ball from the QB through handoffs and look for open lanes to run.

Offensive Line: The offensive line is made up of five linemen: Left Tackle (LT), Left Guard (LG), Center (C), Right Guard (RG), and Right Tackle (RT). These players are positioned along the scrimmage line. Wide receivers are not part of the offensive line even though they are positioned along the scrimmage line on the field. The offensive line's role is to protect the quarterback from being tackled before he can throw the ball. Another of their roles is to open lanes in the defense, which the ball carrier will run.

Players that make up the offensive line are usually the biggest and strongest players on the team.

Wide Receiver (WR): Wide receivers are some of the fastest players on the team. They are positioned along the scrimmage line. Their role is to receive or catch a pass from the quarterback. But wide receivers are not counted as part of the offensive line. This is because their role is different from that of the offensive line. WR is usually the first player whom the quarterback looks for when they get a snap. They occasionally will try to run with the ball downfield.

In some instances, the WR will receive the handoffs. Since they are the ball catchers, they use the gloves to have a firm grip on the ball thrown by the quarterback.

Tight End (TE): The tight end can be positioned in multiple positions depending on the offensive game plan. Often, the TE is positioned on either side of the offensive line behind the scrimmage line. Again, tight ends can be set in wide receiver position, running back, and full back—this will depend on the offensive game plan. You can think of the tight end as the utility player in your team.

Phase 2: The Defensive Concept

When the opposition has the ball, your team now becomes the defense. The aim of defense is to prevent their opponent from scoring touchdowns. In addition, creating takeaways by either an interception or fumble recovery is another essential goal of a top-tier defense. Takeaways can transition into opportunities to score for the defense! The fundamentals of defending are tackling and making turnovers. The defense consists of the following positions:

Defensive Line: The defensive line is the first line of defense positioned on the line of scrimmage opposite the offensive line. The role of the defensive line is to counter the offensive line, narrow the ball carrier's running space, tackle players, and stop them from advancing to the end zone. Lastly, one of the most rewarding plays a defensive lineman can make is to sack the quarterback! Nothing will fire your team up more than sacking the quarterback in the right situation during the game! Usually, teams put stronger and broader players on the defensive line. The defensive line comprises the following positions:

- **Defensive End (DE):** These players are positioned on either side of the field just inside the cornerbacks who are arranged opposite to the offense wide receivers
- **Defensive Tackle (DT):** Players positioned opposite to the offense guards. Depending on the formation, there can only be three or four defensive tackles.

Linebacker (LB): Linebackers are players positioned just behind the defensive line. Teams often feature three or four of them, depending on their defensive formation. A team often fields an outside linebacker (OLB), inside linebacker (ILB), and middle linebacker (MLB). An outside linebacker is positioned behind the defensive end on both sides of the field while the inside linebacker and middle linebacker occupy positions just behind the defensive tackle. The main tasks of linebackers are:

- Tackling or attacking the quarterback
- Preventing the running backs from advancing past the defensive line
- They defend against rushing passes.

Cornerback (CB): Cornerbacks are players positioned opposite to the wide receivers of the offense. They tackle any player on the offense who catches the ball, such as wide receivers, running backs, and tight ends. They are responsible for defending passes or intercepting balls thrown their way. Depending on the play, the field has two to four cornerbacks. These types of players must be strong and capable tacklers.

Safety (S): Safety has two positions in the field: strong safety (SS) and weak safety (WS). These positions differ in that the strong safety is on the strong side of the field while the free safety is on the weak side of the field. Both are placed in the backfield about 15 yards from the scrimmage line. For this reason, they are considered the last line of defense. The strong point of the S players is their passing abilities. The role of the safety is to handle the ball carrier by tackling them on both running and passing play should they break through the defensive line.

Phase 3: Special Teams

Special teams refer to a unit of players who occupy the field during kicking plays. Players in this unit should have special skills. They come onto the field during field goals, kick-offs, and punts. Typically, when one team's special team joins the field, the opposition team's special team also takes the field. A special team consists of the following:

Kicker (K): A special team player responsible for kick-offs and field goals. Kickers usually have powerful legs. It's rare to find accurate kickers in youth football.

Punter (P): The punter's role is to catch and kick the ball away to the defense after the offense fails to get a first down. The kick or punt limits the field position for the defense if they gain possession. Punting is challenging because the punter has to be quick to catch and kick the ball before being tackled. That's why punters are strong and quick players.

Return specialist: Return specialists consist of a punt returner (PR) and kick returner (KR). The returner's role is to return the punt to gain field position for the offense. The kicker or punter kicks the ball to the KR or PR. A return specialist should be agile and able to spot and position themselves to catch the ball.

Long snapper: The long snapper's role is to snap the ball back to the punter or kicker for the field goal or punter's attempt. Long snappers must be strong and active as they need to snap the ball about 15 yards to the punter or kicker. Additionally, a long snapper has to stop the offensive team from blocking the punt or field goal. These players are the integral position of the team, and most are talked about little.

Understanding football positions and their roles is the foundation of coaching youth teams. Knowing this allows you to spot and assign field roles to your players based on their skills. It's a requirement for your team to understand field positions for safe, fun, and enjoyable practice sessions.

TEACHING THE THREE POINT STANCE

When getting ready for a play, players use different stances—the positions they take to get ready for the game to kick off or before the ball gets snapped. There are various stances, including a 2-point stance, a 3-point stance, and a 4-point stance. A stance influences power, speed, explosiveness, and balance. Teaching your youth players correct stances is vital as a coach because an incorrect stance will lead to poor performance. Our focus will be on the 3-point stance since it's the most common.

The Three-Point Stance

The three-point stance technique is important to offensive linemen. It's a quality stance that, when well executed, will allow players to stay balanced and move quickly. Here's how to teach your youth players the three-point stance:

1. **Distance of the feet**: Get your players to plant their feet shoulder-width apart or less on the ground. The aim is to remain balanced. If they spread their feet too wide or too close, opponents will easily push them down. Having one leg slightly back is still correct.
2. **Feet should point ahead:** Tell your players to point their feet straight ahead. This allows the player to move forward swiftly off the ground while maintaining balance.

3. **Bend down nearly to the sitting position:** Get your players to squat down to approximate the sitting position. While in that position, they should put one hand down so that it's just in front of their body and a bit inside the closest foot. They can touch down with any hand.

4. **Body weight:** Ensure that about 70% of a player's weight rests on the hips and feet and 30% on the hand touching the ground. This maximizes power on take-off.

5. **Positioning of the other hand:** Tell your players to rest their remaining hand on their knee or thigh. This arm should bend at the elbow to form an acute angle and be in a position that can be used quickly. Offensive or defensive line players will use the hand early for rushing and blocking moves or hit or whack away their opposition.

6. **Alignment of shoulders parallel to the ground:** Your players should now square their shoulders to the line of scrimmage. Furthermore, the shoulders should be parallel to the ground. Widening the chest creates a larger area for effective blocking.

7. **Head position**: It is crucial to teach your players to keep their heads up while making a

tackle. Players can spot a blitz or stunt when they have their heads up. This is exceptionally important because this can prevent injuries. It can be challenging for children to assume this position, but patience is important when training them.

It's ideal for teaching your players the three-point stance and all basics early. Let your first two practice sessions be about three-point stances because it's fundamental, and players can't perform well without it.

When teaching the kids the basics, some will catch on faster than others. This is where your assistance is of utmost importance. Keeping an eye on all players to see who is struggling or who needs more attention is essential. This also helps you identify the skills of each one of your players. When a player finally gets a play or drill right, find a way to praise them, such as giving them a high five. This helps keep the positive energy within the team and boosts the player's confidence.

SAFETY IN YOUTH FOOTBALL

Football is a beautiful game carved deep into Americans' minds. Football promotes unity and encourages teamwork. However, it is one of the sports full of physical contact that involves tackling, falling, and tumbling. This physical contact can result in injuries. This is where safety equipment and a safety coaching protocol can come in handy.

Safety Equipment for Football

One of the means for protecting players from injuries is the usage of proper safety equipment. The mandatory equipment for this purpose is:

Helmet: This crucial safety equipment protects a player from head injuries when they collide with another player on the field.

Shoulder, hip, though, knee, and butt pads: Protect players from shoulder injuries when they come into close contact with an opponent on the field.

Cleats: They're shoes with spikes for better grip on the ground. Cleats help players avoid sliding and getting injured or injuring other players. They also help players maintain balance.

Mouth guard: Protects a football player from damaging and losing their teeth during tackling.

Important! Ensure that all your players have the right size of safety equipment. Remember to show them how to use each piece of equipment properly.

Safety Coaching Tips to Add to Your Safety Protocol

Football is a beautiful game, but we can't kid ourselves and think it doesn't have challenges. There's no doubt that this beloved game can be dangerous to players. A recent survey by USA Football found that 35% of injuries—the most common—were contusions, followed by ligament sprains at 15% (Matava, 2019). You should take the safety of players to heart in practices and games. The following tips will help your players stay safe:

Implement the latest USA Football regulations: USA Football sets the rules of American youth football to increase the safety of players. For example, it requires players of the same size to line up against each other.

Use certified coaches: Coaches certified by USA Football or the Youth Football Coaches Association have been trained in the safety of players. Using such coaches helps ensure that players stay safe in practices and games. This is particularly important if you still need to be certified.

Get players to practice safe tackling: You'll encounter this idea numerous times throughout this book. I can't emphasize enough that you should teach your players how to tackle safely. The key during tackling is to ensure the head isn't in the line of fire but out to avoid concussions.

Develop a zero-tolerance policy against bad tackles: Do all that's legally allowed to discourage your players from making bad hits and illegal tackles. The game of rugby is known for taking harsh steps against illegal tackles, and you can take a leaf out of it in this respect. If it means that you should bench a player for making bad hits, do so.

Have your players checked by a physician: Parents might need to be made aware that their child has certain health conditions that could be risky when playing Football. Also, a child may have incurred injuries in the previous season while playing for another team. To prevent safety issues during the upcoming season, have players checked by a physician as a precaution.

Talk to parents and players about concussion symptoms: A concussed player often doesn't know much about where they are or may not even know their name. When not spotted timely, the player's health and life are at risk. Teaching players and parents about concussion symptoms help players report possible concussions timely.

Reach out to distracted players: Children can be distracted during practice or games like older players. Reasons for this include life situations, especially at home and school. Distracted players can't focus, which can harm their health. That's why you should know your players to intervene when they appear, not themselves. Remember that you're not raising only great football players but also great people.

Inspect the football field before using it: An uneven field with holes can be hazardous to players. The reason is that players can trip, especially in bad areas where wide receivers run to. Tripping can result in falls that may cause head injuries or damage to ankles.

Appoint a player safety coach: A player coach's role is to encourage safe playing during practices and games. This crucial role ensures players are hydrated and properly wear fitting safety equipment. The player safety coach will keep coaches looking for unsafe practices and acting accordingly.

Include cool-down stretches into practice sessions: After every strenuous activity, ensure that your players stretch. This occasion gives you time to discuss goals for the next exercise and to provide feedback to players after the previous exercise. Cool-down stretches can be short.

Provide enough time for full warm-ups: Warm-ups are crucial to player safety. They prepare the body for the strenuous activities that are still to come. During warm-ups, the body prepares to supply enough oxygen and nutrients to the muscles, reduces stress on joints, and raises the body temperature for enhanced flexibility. Skipping warm-ups might result in injuries and non-optimized performance.

Encourage players to hydrate during practices and games: Water is the main component of blood. When players hydrate, they not only cool their bodies but also facilitates optimal blood flow for proper body functioning and transportation of nutrients. Most importantly, your players will likely avoid muscle cramps, fatigue, and dizziness.

Establish a heat index for your area: It's OK to consider outside temperatures to determine whether it's too hot or not to play. Coaches often need to include humidity in their assessment of outdoor temperatures. A combination of temperature and humidity is called a heat index. When the heat index exceeds 104 degrees, consider stopping play from avoiding fainting or heat stroke.

In concluding this chapter, I'd like to reiterate some important points. You want to be a good coach and build a team of superstars. It's vital, therefore, to encourage teamwork, teach respect, value the safety of players, and instill the value of being human. Teach them to own up to their mistakes without forgetting that it starts with you.

Be on the lookout for players who need to catch up and provide special assistance. Remember to be fun and create a healthy environment for the children so that they feel comfortable.

4

HOW TO PLAN PRACTICES

P roper practice is key to establishing a solid winning team. Proper practice requires proper practice planning. As a coach, it's your job to ensure that you teach your children—players— the fundamentals of Football. The place where your players can learn the fundamentals of Football practically, such as how to perform a legal tackle, is at practice.

Whether you're a beginner or an experienced youth football coach, you need to have a thorough and clear practice plan. Considering the many positions and skills that your players should learn, your practice plan must be well-structured.

Where do you start when creating a well-thought-out practice plan? It begins with the football players that you have. By this time, you should have a roster of your players but you're yet to know much about their skills. A properly planned practice will give you all you need to prepare for and play games.

CONSTRUCT A WRITTEN PRACTICE PLAN

The start of the upcoming season is fast approaching, and so is the first day of practice. What are you going to do on your first day of practice? Youth football has various rules and regulations from youth football governing bodies. Every coach and team has their philosophy, but one thing that all must prioritize: The safety of children. Hence, before starting your first practice, check those regulations and recommendations from youth football governing bodies such as USA Football.

With safety in mind, every head coach must have a practice plan. Here's how to approach practices.

- **Have your practice plan in black and white:** The goals of each practice session are the first item to put down on paper or desired device. It's good to capture practice objectives because it helps focus. Divide your practice plan to cater to 20–30 minutes of station rotations. You don't want to be caught up spending excessive practice on one station because it's fun for the players.

- **Work on weak spots**: Once you know your team's or some players' weaknesses, add drills to your practice plan to work on them. This helps you to work on important skills, even if they may be boring.

- **Dedicate 15 minutes to warm up and huddle:** Warm-up is essential and must be scheduled in your practice plan. During warm-ups, you can discuss many things, such as expectations and introducing new players and coaches.

- **Plan 30 minutes on offense:** If you have 2 hours total practice time, allocate 60 minutes— half of the practice time—to offense. Split this hour into two 30-minute intervals in which you work on individual and team offense.

- **Give 15 minutes to special teams:** Take at most 15 minutes working on special teams. You want to find the best kickers, holders, snappers, and punters here. It's also important to rotate players in this category. The reason for player rotation in every station is to ensure that they are all taking part and to find the best fit for the role.

- **Allocate 30 minutes to defense:** The second-most important area of football coaching is the defense. The 30 minutes allocated are enough to perform targeted drills on a practice day.

WHAT TO FOCUS ON IN THE FIRST TWO WEEKS OF PRACTICE

Equipment fitting: Make sure every player has the right size helmets, shoulder pads, cleats, and mouth guards. Having the right size equipment protects your players from injuries. By focusing on equipment fitting, you're demonstrating that you care about the safety of the children. Here are things that are achievable within two weeks:

Find your center and quarterback: You must identify your center and quarterback as early as possible. The reason is that most offensive plays will revolve around them, especially the quarterback. You are determining who they are early and providing ample time to develop their skills.

Spot your linebackers: Pay attention during tackle drills because that's when you can identify good linebackers.

Go easy on tackling: Tackling is a massive part of the football game. I get it, and everyone close to the game gets it. However, going hard on tackling from the get-go can be a recipe for injuries early in the season. Schedule your first practice as a no-contact session and then half-contact on your third practice. Engage in full contact on the fourth practice session. However, some players may prefer to avoid engaging in hitting. Don't force them to because it might deter them from participating in the sport. Such players may be more suited to kicking and punting.

A practice plan allows coaches and parents to follow your lead. For this reason, you should share your written practice plan with them and the players. Having a practice will also show parents that their children are in capable hands and an organized coach.

SUGGESTIONS FOR RUNNING PRACTICES

What to do to run a safe practice? Here are tips for running your practice successfully:

Set up multiple drill stations: Bad player behaviors can surface quickly if idle. Instead, keep all your players busy by setting up multiple drill stations. Every player will have something to do, which means your players have a chance to learn new skills faster. Also, multiple drill stations allow you to focus on teaching multiple skills at a go.

Speed up practice: Running 15–20 minutes per station allows children to have more breaks and is easy to keep practice fun. If you have planned a 30-minute station, break it up into two 15-minute periods.

End session with fun activity: After a heavy practice session, you don't want to hear your players complaining about the session's toughness. This may stress them and make them think twice about coming to the next practice. If you follow a tough practice session with a fun activity at the end, players leave the field enthused and felt like keeping on playing Football.

Demonstrate drills: The best and most effective teaching method is demonstration performance. You do what you are teaching and explain why you are doing it. Children learn faster by watching rather than by just listening. If you can't demonstrate a technique or skill, get someone to do so on your behalf. Another option is to show players films before they try a skill or technique on the field. A film doesn't have to be long. Great videos on places like YouTube run for less than two minutes.

Be the first to arrive at practice and last to leave: Children and adults learn by copying someone. This learning occurs subconsciously, which is how we learn our native languages. If you arrive first at training, many players and parents will copy you. That's great because they'll be simulating a great habit. As soon as players arrive, get to work. Be the last person to leave the field to ensure every player's parent has fetched their child.

EVALUATE YOUR PLAYERS WEEKLY

How do you know if your players are improving in specific skill sets, such as tackling, blocking, agility, and passing? Many youth football coaches try to rely on memory and end up being biased in evaluating their players. It's even more challenging when you have to explain to the parents of a specific player why they're not starting. The solution is to have a weekly player evaluation system.

It doesn't have to be a complex system; a simple spreadsheet will do. With this system, you can rank players weekly based on how they execute certain skills. For example, you can rank players on tackling by allocating points ranging from one to five, with five being excellent. The low-scoring players will need extra attention at practice to sharpen their skills and technique in that particular aspect of Football. You can also spot the players making progress from week to week.

It would be best if you shared your notes and evaluations with your coaching staff. Be mindful of what information you share with all the parents, especially parents whose children need extensive remedial work. For such parents, invite them to a meeting and discuss the child's performance and your plans to help them improve.

For objective evaluations, it's best to study the films you take during practices and games. These videos could be helpful when discussing improvement areas with your player's parents and the player. Most importantly, your evaluation chart helps you develop an effective practice plan for future sessions.

WHAT YOU NEED TO CARRY IN YOUR COACHING BAG

To execute your practice plan, you must practice well-prepared for the session. You need to organize two bags to protect sensitive equipment like cameras: a coaching bag and an equipment bag. Bags do not have any influence on the team's performance. You save time when you have all the football equipment in place.

If you mix your team playbook with cones, agility bags, and footballs, soon, the playbook will wear out and become unusable. Remember that players watch and learn from you. As a result, pack your bags in an organized manner so your players can copy how to be organized. With that in mind, let's discuss some items to pack in the two bags mentioned above.

ITEMS IN THE TEAM'S EQUIPMENT BAG: ITEMS IN THE COACH'S BAG

Items in the Team's Equipment Bag	Items in the Coach's Bag
Cones	Roster
Scrimmage caps	Playbook
Balls	Camera
Kicking tees	Pen and pencils
Athletic tape	Notebook
Football first aid kit	Team playbook
Football pants	Drill sheets
Agility rings	Practice plan
Hand shields	One or two mouthpieces
Half round bags	Player sign-up forms
King crab sled	Mini white board
Medium erase board	League rules

Pay attention to the importance of having organized bags. It's like having all kitchen or garage items well-organized. You don't want to run all over the house when you want a wrench. If you do, soon you'll be stressed. A stressed coach is unlikely to enthuse players on the football field, and you can't have a great practice session.

THE IMPORTANCE OF GOOD MANAGEMENT IN PRACTICES

The team's performance hugely depends on the type of management, from the head to assistant coaches to top players. Good management ensures that practice goes according to plan. And when this happens, you can be sure that the team will perform well.

What does it mean by good youth football management? It starts with the head coach. When the head coach crafts practice plans, all the other coaches will do as well. As a result, you can expect organized practice sessions, a requirement for effective teaching and learning. If you pay attention to schoolteachers, you'll notice that those with teaching plans have organized classes in which children learn better. The same goes for teaching youth football.

No player will be idling in practice as the scripted practice plan will demand to have all the children busy at any given time. There'll be high energy and enthusiasm in practices run by exemplary managers, which children enjoy. Good management also means that the coaching staff is on the same page, which leads to teamwork in practices and games.

Good managers not only manage assistant coaches but also know how to manage parents and players. Most importantly, they're confident and stick to their beliefs even in tough times because they know their football system works.

Any coach or manager who doesn't do or has the qualities above is considered a bad manager. It's rare for such managers to win games and to develop great players. Resolve to be a good manager and do what these types of people do on and off the football field.

SCOUTING IS A PART OF WINNING

How do you prepare a game plan against opponents you know little about? The answer is to scout the opponent and their top players. Carefully selected scouts carry out this task. Not only do these individuals collect information about the opponents, but they also look for potential signings.

Scouts attend and watch games involving their future opponents to do this important job. In some cases, they watch films of games involving the coming opponent. During the game, they collect information such as the best players in defense and offense, the opponent's best plays, and identify special teams. Scouting is complete once you understand your opponent's weaknesses and strengths. That's why scouting is often followed by analyzing the opponent and their players. Once all this information is ready, scouts hand it to the coaches for practice and game planning.

How to Scout, the Opponent

The best way to know your football opponent better is through thorough scouting. It allows you to identify their weak and strong points, which is crucial for planning games. Here is a guide on scouting your opponent.

Step 1 - Be organized: When time allows, it's important to watch games involving your opponents. Before leaving for the game, ensure that you're organized. This means you know your objectives for watching the game and have the right tools, including pencils, a clipboard, scouting sheets, a legal pad, and a stopwatch.

Step 2 - Arrive early at the game: It's always a good idea to arrive early before the game starts. This allows you to watch how your opponents warm up, and you get to know players by name and number. Ideally, come earlier than both teams.

Step 3 - Find a better viewing spot: A great view of the whole field is crucial. Only sit where your view will be obscured to avoid missing essential plays. That way, you'll see all the players and plays. Be prepared and focus on the following:

- **Opponent's offense tendencies**: How they align when they have the ball, how fast they move it, and how they manage the clock.
- **Formations:** How they set up and execute their plays.
- **Defensive tendencies:** How the opponent aligns themselves when they defend.

Special teams: Check the team's coverages and how they execute their kicks and field goals. How powerfully do they kick the ball? When you check this, record how long it takes for kickers to kick the Football.

Step 4 - Player information: Identify and look closely at five top defensive and five offensive players. Get their names, height, size, and speed. This information will allow you to create a solid game plan.

Step 5 - Identify weak and strong points: This is crucial for your game plan. When you know your opponents' strengths, you can practice how to defend against them well ahead of time. Coupled with their weak points, you can have an overall game plan that best uses your team's strong points.

Step 6 - Plan around your findings: Now that you've gathered the information needed, it's time to develop a plan. Your plan should include how you'll practice defense and offense drills.

As you can see, scouting can make a difference in your practice plans and how you approach games. Take it seriously. If you can't access videotapes of your opponent's games, record your own if the league allows.

CLOCK MANAGEMENT

Other than scouting your opponent's strategic plays in defense and offense, it would be best to consider another critical aspect of a game: clock management. In Football, you face your opponent and have to deal with time. There are situations in Football where time becomes the most important factor to use effectively. The leading team often implements plays during a football game to minimize playtime. On the other hand, the trailing team usually calls plays targeted at saving time and increasing scoring opportunities.

How does the Football clock work? It's necessary, therefore, that you understand clock management. This is where the rules of youth football come in.

The Rules of the Clock in the Football Game

Upon starting the game, the clock starts counting down when the receiving team player touches or catches the ball and runs with it from their end zone to the opponents'. The clock will count down until an event leads to its stoppage. The first scenario is when the offense's play ends. Once the quarterback snaps the ball, the clock runs again and will only stop when:

- The ball carrier runs out of bounds.
- One of the teams calls a timeout or the officials call a timeout such as when there's an injured player on the field.
- Either team scores a touchdown or when there's a field goal kick or penalty.
- The official rule is that a pass is incomplete.
- It's the end of the game. The team attacking the play is not stopped until the ball is declared dead.

Practice Clock Management

Youth football teams often attempt to quicken or slow the clock depending on the score between them. They make use of different strategic plays to achieve their desired goal. When scouting your opponents, learning how they manage the clock is vital. Most importantly, you want your defense and offense to have the same mindset regarding clock management.

A savvy youth football coach will include clock management drills in their practice plan. The reason is that they're aware of the possible situations where time becomes precious. During clock management drills, one of your coaches starts and stops them while another man's the clock to announce the clock status.

Here are two important drills to perform in practice. The aim of these drills is two-fold: to teach players how to handle plays when time is a factor and to drill them on the importance of the clock use during the game.

The two-minute drill: In this drill, the offense is trailing and would want to move the ball quickly to score to win the game. In this drill, have a coach signal the end of plays and another announce the remaining time. The offense snaps the ball as soon as the 20-second period begins. There should be no resets or pauses, just as in games near the end of the half or end of the game. The offense should avoid being tackled inbound and run out of bounds for the clock to stop. The defense, in contrast, should try to keep the ball carrier in bounds.

The one-minute drill: This drill is suitable when the offense is trailing and time of significant concern—they have one minute to score to win or level the game. They need to score and do so quickly. In this drill, the offense practices to get on with play as fast as possible. They move down the field as quickly as possible. At the same time, the defense should align quickly and try to tackle the ball carrier. If the defense manages to tackle and stop the offense, the coach whistles for the end of the game, and the defense wins.

Incorporating these drills into your weekly practices will improve your team's performance and instill the importance of clock management under pressure.

5

TEN COMMON DRILLS EACH ON OFFENSE, DEFENSE, AND SPECIAL TEAMS

The way to learn football skills is through drills—repeating a skill repeatedly until players execute it almost automatically. Drills are crucial when learning new skills at any football level, especially for beginner players at youth levels. In that light, this chapter focuses on a few drills on offense, defense, and special teams. The aims of these drills at youth football levels are to:

- Build the fundamentals
- Help young players to execute the basics in a game situation
- Develop technical and tactical skills needed to accelerate a team's improvement

- Put young players in positions to succeed during the game

OFFENSIVE DRILLS

A strong offense improves a team's chances of scoring touchdowns. During practices, your players learn what to do or not do while on offense. This is where offense drills are so helpful. Let's review ten offense drills to help your team have a strong offense.

1. The QB Pop Pass Drill

The QB pop pass drill is one of the best drills in youth football. It trains young players how to catch and throw the ball. Furthermore, it teaches your QB and center how to work with each other on exchanges. You can use the QB pop pass drill as a warm-up drill and allow latecomers (I don't encourage this, but it happens) to join with minimal interruption. Your QBs must arrive on time, which is key in executing this drill well.

The QB pop pass drill requires two sets of players consisting of 6 to 10 individuals. Each set must have a QB, center, and receivers standing opposite each other and are 15–10 yards. The receivers run to catch a pass from the QB and take the route to the other station. Here, they switch lines to execute another similar run to come back.

Other fundamentals this drill teaches are shot-gun/under center snaps, route running, and throwing and catching. Try to get 20–25 route running scenarios to cement QB/center exchanges.

2. QB-Hip Rotation Throws on One Knee and When Standing Drills

The second drill focuses on QB stances when throwing the ball. The first stance we'll look at is when the QB throws the ball when standing. This drill teaches the QB how to have a great upper body rotation when throwing the ball. This stance allows QBs to generate power when throwing the ball.

Here's how to go about executing this drill. Have two pairs of QBs stand opposite facing each other. Their toes must face their partner, feet at shoulder width apart, and bend the knees slightly. Have the QB holding the holding rotate their upper body until their non-throwing shoulder faces their partner, which is their target. At this point, the arm carrying the ball should be straight up so that the ball is above head height.

The QB now throws the ball to their target while rotating their upper body back. At the point of release, the ball-throwing shoulder must face its target.

The big idea is to train QBs to use their upper body rotation instead of their legs when throwing the ball. This gives them better ball releases and more power.

The second stance is when the QB puts their throwing side knee on the ground. This drill is called the straight arm drill. It aims to train QBs to have high ball releases during throws. Elbows should be as straight as possible. Their partners should have their hands up to give the throwing QB a target. The ball-carrying QB throws the ball to the target.

3. The QB Hand-Off Drill

Ball exchanges between the running back and QB are essential for the offense to gain yards toward the opponent's end zone. For this, it should be carried out seamlessly to avoid turnovers.

The running back can either approach the QB on their left or right side. Let's suppose the running back runs toward the QB on their right side in this drill. The running back starts the drill from a two-point stance with both hands on slightly bent knees. As soon as they start running, they place the arm closest to the QB above the shirt number and the other hand below the shirt number. This way, the running back creates a pocket in which the QB puts the ball.

The QB turns and slots the ball in the running back's pocket, clamps the ball with both arms, and continues running forward. This drill prevents ball exchange mistakes when the running back reaches out for the ball with their hands.

4. The RB Bag Agility Drill

The running back bag agility drill is excellent for getting your players warmed up, but it is even more important to practice correct ball handling. You also want your RBs to be agile, which is another reason to perform this drill. Here's how you go about doing this drill:

- Place three bags about a yard apart.
- Put a cone about five yards from the first bag and a few feet to the side.
- When you blow the whistle, the RB runs and puts a leg into the hole between the first and second bag. Then, to the next hole before exploding forward at speed at the end.
- The RB returns to the start block to perform another rep.
- Get your RB to repeat this process but tap in the hole with two legs to do so faster.
- The RB repeats the drill, tapping with three legs per hole.

Notes: Ensure that the RB looks downfield instead of looking at the bags when performing the drill. Additionally, they should raise their knees as high as possible when tapping in the holes. The ball must be held high and tight all the time.

The third type of agility drill attacks the holes between the bags from the side. Players need to keep their hips low. This exercise works on the inside of the groin. Here's how the activity works:

- A player stands close to the bag facing parallel to it.
- They reverse and attack the space between the first and second bags. Then stop within the hole and pedal back to exit the hole.
- The player repeats the process to the next hole. After exiting the last hole, they burst downfield.

You can do several reps before changing from one agility drill to the next.

5. *The RB Cone Drill*

The cone drill teaches running backs the change of direction and how to be effective. Like the other RB drills covered so far, this one provides good practice for adequately handling the ball. Here's how to take your players through the drill:

- Place three cones in a straight line and about 10 yards apart.
- Position a cone halfway between the first and second cones but offset five yards to the left. Place another cone the same way but between the second and third cones.
- Blow the whistle to start the drill.
- A running back runs from the first cone to the first offset cone, back to the second cone, to the second offset cone, and back to the third cone and bursts downfield. The player should stay on the offset cones. They extend their left leg to the cone and change direction.

Make a couple of reps for each RB before changing to the next drill. In the second part of this drill, the RBs repeat the above process but run around each cone.

6. The WR Stance Drill

It's crucial to solidify the basics or nothing else will work. One of the fundamentals to entrench is the WR stance. This drill will help you with that stance.

- The inside foot and outside foot should be forward and back, respectively.
- Get the WR to shift most of their body weight on the front foot to take off swiftly and to

prevent defenders from knocking you back.

- The WR should keep their hands up and be ready to push off defenders.
- Get the WR to keep their shoulders square to be unpredictable about where they'll go.
- The WR should keep looking at the line of scrimmage to track the ball's release and anticipate its movement.

7. The WR Over the Shoulder Drill

One of the fundamental techniques for wide receivers is catching the ball over the shoulder. This drill aims to strengthen this basic of football. Here's how to go about doing it.

- Split receivers into two groups.
- Align the two groups on hash marks: the first group is on the right hash mark while the second group positions on the left.
- Following the QB's cadence, the WR takes a specific route.
- The QB drops back a few feet and throws the ball over the WR's outside shoulder for them to catch it.

The QB will alternate between the two groups and the WR.

8. The O-Lineman Stance Technique Drill

Balance is critical for offensive line players. An imbalance can't be effective when blocking the defense. I've previously explained how to execute a proper three-point stance. You should train your offensive line relentlessly about the proper stance throughout the season. It may be the right time to review the three-point stance discussed in Chapter 3.

9. The Run Blocking Drills

The offensive line's ability to block the defense can be a difference between scoring touchdowns and conceding football possession. Three things are necessary to execute an effective run block: good stance, power, solid run blocking style, and a fast take-off. Most importantly, an offensive player must learn to finish the block.

The run blocking drill I'm about to share with you is fun, and your children will enjoy it. Here's how you execute it.

- Use cones to create five yards by five yards box.
- Have two players position themselves on opposite sides of the box.
- Tell your players to bend at the knees and be straight as possible at the waist for maximum

strength. This sinks the hips and creates leverage.

- Blow the whistle to start the drill. The players will get off and block each other until one wins the duel, or you blow the whistle after a couple of seconds.

Important: Pair the players so that the duels can be competitive.

10. The Pass Blocking Drills

The pass blocking drill teaches your offensive line players the proper technique to set and deliver a punch to slow rushing defenders. It'll teach them speed and explosion to protect a pass. You don't want your offensive line players to step backward and be run over by the defense. Here's how to drill your players in this technique.

- Place three offensive players on the line in normal formation.
- Align three defensive players across each offensive player. Each defender should hold a hand shield.
- Get your offensive players to assume proper stances to generate explosive power during take-off.

- Blow the whistle to kick off the drill.
- The offensive line players should pass block the defense, ensuring they deliver powerful and tight elbows to the bags.

This drill provides opportunities to test your players on proper stances.

DEFENSIVE DRILLS

Tackling can make or break a football team's performance. Yet, some take it for granted. It doesn't matter how well you prepare your team and how dedicated your players are in practice; if they miss tackles on game day, opponents will outscore you. Check out professional football games, and you'll be convinced that tackling is football's most important defensive skill.

It's essential, therefore, to teach your young players the basics of tackling. The following ten drills will help you develop great tackling players.

1. Shoulder Tackling, Dummies/Sleds, Tackle Wheels, and Pursuit Drills

Shoulder tackling is used by many teams and endorsed by USA Football, the national governing body of amateur football, and Pop Warner, a former American football coach at many institutions. With shoulder tackling, players take their heads out of action, which helps keep head injuries low. Here's how to tackle successfully using this technique.

Tell your tackler to swoop to balance before tackling the ball carrier. Then, they raise their head and eyes so that they can use the front of the shoulder to tackle. To secure the tackle, the player should place their head to the side and out of contact before throwing double uppercuts and grabbing the opponent's jersey. Finally, they explode through the hips to generate power and drive through the ball carrier to complete the tackle.

When training children in proper tackling techniques, it's worth considering using tackling dummies or sleds. This limits your players' live contact in practice and injuries. You can have children run, hit, wrap up, and drive blocking sleds. Tackle wheels can also be used during non-contact drills to improve or teach tackling techniques. Just make sure you get the correct sizes.

Another drill you can use to sharpen the defense is the pursuit drill. This drill begins by setting up the defense in their base alignment. You can have one of the coaches as the ball carrier and have the defense swarm to him. As soon as you signal the start of the pursuit, all the players will try to get to the ball carrier and break down. Having other coaches try to block the defense players can add competitiveness and excitement to the drill.

Although I encourage tackling dummies, remember to do live tackling once or twice a week. However, I suggest you initially focus on non-contact drills until you see the children ready to tackle live.

2. The Lift Drill

To tackle effectively, players shouldn't focus mainly on creating big hits but on how they position and use their bodies. The lift drill is the basic football tackling drill to teach players the proper tackling form. Here's how to run this drill.

You need to have two players: one to tackle and another as a ball carrier. Get them to line up facing each and standing five yards apart. Blow the whistle to initiate the drill. The tackler will begin to run at the ball carrier. It's important to do this at half speed so every player can understand the drill.

At a point where the tackler can contact the ball carrier, they use their hips to explode into the ball carrier. Then they rise and club their hands around the ball carrier. Simultaneously, they should grab the ball carrier's jersey and lift them off the ground. To affect the lift drill, the ball carrier should jump into the air when the tackler reaches them to make it easy for the tackler to pick them off the ground. Finally, the tackler should gently drive the ball carrier for about five yards and put them back on the ground.

3. *The Angle Tackling Drill*

Some drills teach players how to tackle a player head-on. Sometimes such tackles aren't effective because of the unavailability of opportunities to do so, especially in game situations. The angle tackle may be the only option available as the ball carrier tries to prevent being wrapped up. Your players should be prepared to handle such situations. Here's how to teach your players how to angle tackle:

You need three cones and two players. Place the first two cones 10 yards apart and in front of each player. Form an equilateral triangle of cones by placing the third cone 10 yards apart from each of the first two cones.

When you blow the whistle, the offensive player runs on the outside toward the third cone. The defensive player runs the same way on their side. While running, the defensive player should keep their eyes on the offensive player while their shoulders stay square all the time.

As the two players near the top of the triangle, the defensive player should put their body and helmet in front of and across the offensive player and their numbers. Immediately the defensive player reaches the ball carrier, they sink their hips and explode while running through it. The tackler should keep driving the ball carrier while their helmet remains in front of the offensive player.

Remember to carry out this drill at half speed to avoid injuries. The idea is not to make big hits but to teach your players how to angle tackle.

4. The Linebacker Lateral Movement Drill

The linebacker lateral movement drill teaches the defense that the sideline can be an additional defender. Defenders can use the sideline to their advantage by forcing ball carriers to the outside of the field. The sideline can make it easier to tackle players or force ball carriers to run over it.

You need three cones to perform this drill. Place two cones about five yards apart along the sideline of your choice. Form a triangle by positioning the third cone about five yards from the sideline and halfway between the first two cones. The triangle so formed will act as the playing field.

Have the ball carrier and defender line up five yards back from the third cone and face each other. They must be about 10 yards from each other. When you blow the whistle to start the drill, the ball carrier runs toward the sideline portion inside the triangle. Simultaneously, the tackler runs toward the ball carrier. Both players must always stay within the triangle.

The focus of the tackler should be to angle the ball carrier toward the sideline and avoid letting them escape toward the infield. When the ball carrier turns up field toward the sideline, the tackler prepares themselves to tackle. They wrap up the ball carrier as soon they get to the point of contact.

5. *The Linebacker Mirror Drill*

The linebacker mirror drill teaches the defense how to pursue ball carriers downfield while maintaining their eyes on them.

You need to have six cones to perform this drill. Place the cones in a straight line, so they're a few feet apart. Arrange to have two groups of players: ball carriers and tacklers.

- Line up one player from each group to the left of the first cone, so they're five yards apart and face each other.
- Blow the whistle to start the drill.

- The ball carrier runs down the line of cones while holding the ball with the arm away from the tackler.
- Get the tackler to mirror the run of the ball carrier on his side of the cones. When they recognize the ball carrier making a cut upfield, they should angle their body, cut the ball carrier off, and tackle them following the angle tackle technique.

6. The One v One Pass Rush Drill

Undoubtedly, the quarterback is the most important player on the football field. A strong pass rusher is arguably the second-most crucial position. It's, therefore, essential to work on pass rush skills during youth football practices. As a youth football coach, you're in an enviable position in that most of your players will play either defense or offense. The one vs. one pass rush drill will help strengthen both your defense and offensive players.

To execute this drill, you need a defensive line player and an offensive line player. Line up both players in their respective field positions. Have the offensive line player imitate pass blocking during a game to protect the defensive line from reaching and tackling the quarterback within five to six seconds.

Rotate players to allow every player to play offense and defense during the drill. Preferably, use two defensive line and two offensive line players simultaneously to have more active players.

7. The Shuffle, Angle, and Pedal Drill

Defensive backs need the right footwork to intercept passes or tackle offensive wide receivers. Teaching this to your youth football players will set the foundation for success when these children reach high school or higher levels. Here's how to perform this drill:

- Position 3–4 players five yards apart, preferably on field lines. Each player should take an angled stance in anticipation of a run-pass option (RPO).
- When you blow the whistle to start the drill, the lined-up players begin a slow three-step shuffle back.
- Once the three-step is cleared, the players transition into a fast backpedal with their hips down and shoulders over the knees.
- At the top of the top, you simulate a ball thrown short.
- Players should now dig their back cleats into the ground and burst up field to prepare to

tackle the offense. When going up field, the players do so at an angle.

The variation of the above drill teaches players to anticipate and cut off a deep-threat wide receiver. Instead of bursting forward after the shuffle back, the defensive players take a 45-degree down the field.

8. The Ball Tip Drill

The ball tip drill is one of the most well-known defensive drills used at various football levels, including the National Football League (NFL). It's mainly used for defensive backs, but you can involve linebackers and the defensive line. All it takes is having the football and two defensive players. It's a simple drill to execute.

- One player runs from the sideline along a line while the second follows behind them, so the players are about two yards apart. The coach stands a couple of yards from the starting point of these players.
- The coach tosses the ball to the first player above his head. This player, in turn, tips the ball over to their oncoming partner.
- The oncoming player catches the ball and completes his run toward the coach.

You can adjust the ball tip drill at each practice. For example, you can perform the drill at the line of scrimmage in one practice and shift to deep passes during the next practice.

9. The Forced Fumble and Recovery Drill

Forcing turnovers and taking care of the football on offense can significantly affect your season performance. Turnovers can be the difference between winning and losing games. An article by the Harvard Sports Analysis Collective revealed that from 2002 to 2013, football teams with one more turnover than their opponents won 69.6% of the games (Ryan, 2014).

The forced fumble and recovery drill aims to help your team to keep the ball on offense. It can also be a great warm-up exercise that involves all your players. It would be best if you had footballs and three bags to perform the forced fumble and recovery drill.

- Place three bags parallel to each other and about a yard apart. The players are going to shuffle over and be perpendicular to these bags.
- Position yourself five yards from the last bag and a yard to its right. The players are going to face you when shuffling over the bags.
- Get one player to stand next to the first bag facing you with bent knees, waist, and eyes up.

- Blow the whistle to kick off the drill.
- The player will shuffle through the bags as fast as possible while looking up.
- As they near the end of the last bag, throw them the ball so it touches the ground before reaching them.
- The player should catch the ball and burst toward an assistant coach located a yard or two on your side.
- If a player fumbles the ball, they should recover it by diving and protecting it with their body.

10. The DB Line Drill

You should get your players to practice often. The defensive back-line drill teaches your defense multiple techniques, including plant and explode, backpedal, and run for a touchdown. Here's how the drill works.

- A defensive player starts from the sideline and backpedals for about five yards.
- They stop and burst forward.
- You throw the ball to them, and they catch it and continue to run toward the sideline.

SPECIAL TEAMS

1. *The Kickoff Coverage Drill*

- During kickoffs or punts, you want your special teams to be disciplined and stay in position. This kickoff coverage drill helps achieve that aim. Here's how this drill works.
- Place two kickoff coverage players on one sideline so that they're 10 yards apart. For example, one player will be on the 10-yard line and another on the 20-yard line.
- Position a kickoff returner on the opposite sideline, halfway between the two kickoff coverage players. In this case, the returner will be on the 15-yard line.
- The two kickoff coverage players burst forward when you blow the whistle to start the drill.
- Immediately the coverage players reach the first hash marks; the returner begins to run toward them. Once they get to the second hash mark, the kickoff returner may run anywhere they want. In this example, the 'sidelines' for the returner are the goal line and the 40-yard line.
- The coverage players keep running as they get closer to the returner. In the process, they should keep the returner between them.

Important: The kickoff coverage players should keep their hips and shoulder parallel to the kickoff returner.

2. The Kickoff Lane Tackle Drill

The kickoff lane drill teaches discipline in staying in position during kickoff coverage and making an open field tackle. Here's how this drill works:

- The tackler begins on the numbers and sprints to the first hash mark avoiding the first blocker.
- They get back to their lane and again, avoiding the blocker. This should happen as fast as possible.
- The returner runs left or right, and the tackler wraps up and makes the tackle.

3. The Cross Face Tackle Drill

The cross-face tackle drill teaches how to avoid blockers and make a safe open field tackle. It works as follows:

- A tackler begins at a cone and sprints five yards.
- The coach assigns the blocker who goes at the tackler.
- The tackler gives a move and finds the returner.
- The returner goes left or right, and the tackler wraps up and drives them back.

It's advisable to stress the importance of saving tackle.

4. The Punt Block Hand Placement Drill

The special team's punt block hand placement drill teaches the correct hand placement when blocking a punt. Here's how to run this drill:

- Have a defender stand one yard from you and motion their hands as if they're running.
- Hold the football and act as if to punt it.
- The defender should place their hands on the block point and block the ball.

You should primarily focus on the correct placement of the defender's hand because this drill is already minimal.

5. The Kickoff Return Blocking Drill

The special teams kickoff return blocking box drill teaches the attack-style frontline attack to your kickoff frontline players. This drill can be performed as a whole group or one at a time. Here's how to do the drill:

- Use cones to make 10 yards by 10 yards boxes.
- Have an offensive player stand three to four yards from one end of the box.

- Position a defensive player at the left or right cone closest to the offensive player.
- The offensive player runs straight using the attack-style frontline attack. Blow the whistle to kick off the drill.
- Immediately, the defensive player enters the box and assumes a proper stance to block the offensive player. The objective is to continue with the block until the whistle blows.
- The offensive player locks up with the defender and tries to force them to the sideline.

6. The Half Line Field Goal Drill

The half-line field goal drill teaches the steps and proper assignments of the field goal team members. It's vital to do this drill rapidly to get in the maximum number of reps and to accustom the kicker, holder, and snapper to pressure.

Defenders shouldn't cheat by going around the offense. To execute this drill, the holder places the football at the half line for the kicker to kick it through the goalposts. Give each kicker three kicking opportunities before rotating to the next spot.

Get your assistant coaches to spread around to ensure each group performs its responsibilities. Also, ensure that you have at least 12 balls.

7. The Run the Hoop Drill

The aim of the run-the-hoop drill is to teach special teams the correct path when attempting to block a punt. For proper execution of this drill, one player at a time will try to block the punt. Let's see how this drill works.

- Divide players into three groups and let them align on the 15-yard line. Use bell dummies or dots to mark the group divisions.
- Assign the punter role to a coach to ensure that defenders block the football properly. This coach punts from the 5-yard line and opposite the main group of players.
- Place hoops two or three yards from the outside groups.
- When you blow the whistle to start the drill, the players run around the hoop and head straight to the block point of the punt.

Ensure that the defense doesn't run into the punter and that they place their hands correctly.

8. The Shoot Tackle Drill

The special teams shoot tackle drill teaches how to make a safe open field tackle on kickoff coverage or punt. Here's how you perform the drill.

- The returner and tackler stand two yards apart.
- When the returner moves, the tackler forms up.
- The tackler grabs and drives their legs to finish the tackle.

Ensure that players assume correct tackling positions. The drill works well when one player goes at a time.

9. The Mirror Tackle Drill

The special teams mirror tackle drill teaches patience and how to make a safe open field tackle. Let's go through how to execute this drill.

- Mark a dot and place two cones five yards from and on both sides of it.
- Both the tackler and returner run to the dot and break down.
- The returner shuffles left and right.
- When you blow the whistle, the tackler runs through the returner and makes a tackle.

10. The Punt Protection Bucket Step Drill

- You teach the special team punt protection bucket step to ensure proper punt protection blocking. Here's how you go about performing this drill.

- Line up defenders in the gap.
- The offensive line players take bucket steps which cut off the defenders and force them into the shields.
- The offensive line players continue up the field for five yards.

Drills are crucial for developing proper techniques. I've covered a small portion of available drills for successfully coaching youth football. You can access more drills and supplemental material on usafootball.com, YouTube, and online coaching courses. You may also refer to the following sites for additional drills to help coach your team:

- https://www.football-tutorials.com/dir/youth-football-drills/
- https://www.shakopeefootball.com/coach-toolkit

6

HOW TO COACH OFFENSE

The offense is a crucial element of football because it controls the balls and scores touchdowns. When in offense, the opponent is simply on the back foot. This doesn't mean that defense isn't important. If you don't score more points than your opponents, it doesn't matter how well you defend. It's true that if you don't concede points, you won't lose games, but it's equally correct to say that if you can't score you can't win games.

At this point, you'll focus on offense before learning how to defend effectively. It's time to teach your young-sters to dominate the opponent's defense and score touchdowns. I will teach you everything about coaching the offense and winning the game in this chapter. You will learn things to look at when designing your offense and when and how to call plays.

WHAT TO CONSIDER WHEN DESIGNING YOUR OFFENSE

As I mentioned throughout, your roster is the starting point of designing any youth football offense. Every football position and scheme you choose largely depends on the skill sets of your players. When creating a powerful offense, you should also consider other elements. Here are more details about what you need.

Chosen offense scheme: There are numerous youth football schemes, including Wing T and Pro-Spread offenses. Your job is to pick a scheme suited to the type of players you have and your football philosophy.

Experience: Your players' experience counts greatly in youth football or any level of football. For example, you can only run heavy plays when your offense consists of new players.

Skill level: Closely related to experience is the skill level of your offense. The skills your players possess influence the type of formation you play. For example, a triple-option offense will only be effective if you have speedy running backs.

Time: The time available to prepare for games limits the number and types of offensive drills you can practice. This calls for you to understand the schemes you choose and how long it takes to teach them to your players. If a scheme takes longer than you can afford, go for alternatives. The rule of thumb is that if you need more time to run it in practice, save time running it in a game. Conversely, if you don't plan to run a scheme in a game, don't practice it.

YOUTH FOOTBALL OFFENSIVE PLAY CALLING STRATEGY

In football, the coaching staff participates in the decisions about what to play to execute next. This involvement is called play calling. Every football coach must have an offensive play calling strategy suitable for their players and likely to lead to scoring points. This is where having a variety of plays that your players understand can put the opponent's defense under pressure most of the time in a game. Your plays should be simple because difficult ones will be hard for your players to execute.

When coaching children, use as simple language as possible. That would assist them in grasping your offensive play calling strategy fast. This is especially important, considering play calls are often a combination of numbers and words. Practicing your offensive play calling will enhance their effectiveness during the game. Here are important guidelines when devising an offensive play calling strategy.

- Keep things simple.
- Pass or handoff the ball to the best offensive player on your team.
- Call off-tackle plays if the sweep is proving to be ineffective.

THE IMPORTANCE OF SCOUTING OPPONENTS' DEFENSE

Scouting is an integral part of planning for practices and games. You can only have an effective offense if you know what your opponent's defense has in store. Your offense play calling strategy is unlikely to work because you might make a call that plays the game into your opponents' hands. The big question is how to scout your opponent's defense using film. The following questions will guide you on what to look for:

- What is their base defense? How do they line up? Diagram their base defenses and include the defensive players' names, ages, numbers, weights, and heights. How do they react to the motion?

- What defensive front do they play, odd or even?
- Who is their best blocker or tackler? Linebacker, line player, or defensive back?
- Who is the weakest player in their defense?
- Who is their dangerous and threatening player?
- What are their defense tendencies?
- What are their most effective plays?
- Does misdirection play confuse them?
- Does their defense line shift when the offense line is unbalanced?
- How aggressive are their linebackers?
- Does the defensive end box or play tight on line reading QB?
- Where and how does the corner adjust to splits, tights, and overloads?
- Where and how does the defensive tackle line up in the C-gap (off-tackle)?
- What is the depth of their inside linebackers and safety?
- Do they blitz much, and whom do they blitz?

Think of other defensive aspects to evaluate. Based on your findings from the film analysis, develop appropriate plays you believe will be effective against your opponent's defense. Try to come up with six or seven offensive plays. Preferably, your offense plays should attack your opponent's defensive weakness—usually, it's one or two incorrectly lined up players.

The most effective way for your players to execute designed plays accordingly is through practice. Put your designed plays into practice and run them.

EIGHT KEY OFFENSE FORMATIONS

The key to dominating and winning the game is scoring more points than the opposition. Scoring points and dominating the game are made possible by using a strong offensive formation. There are many formations and plays associated with each. Let's look at eight offensive formations you can employ.

1. The I Formation

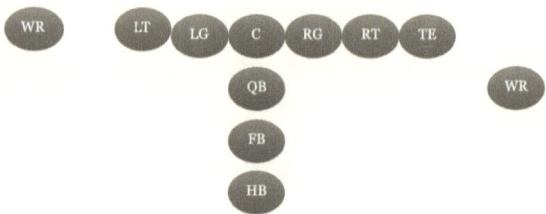

The I formation is one of the commonly used offensive formations in youth football because it's easy to implement. This formation features five offensive line players: two left tackles, two guards, and a center. Behind the center, there's a quarterback, fullback, and halfback along a straight line perpendicular to the line of scrimmage. The benefits of the I formation include:

- **Easy implementation and installation:** It can be installed in a few practices, which is ideal for youth football players. Because it's rare to find strong running backs in youth football, this formation can be a lifesaver. It allows you to field one or two running backs for flexibility.
- **It's run heavy:** This makes the I formation ideal when you plan to run your opponents.
- **Suitable for 'blast' plays:** The I formation supports blast plays where two lead blockers are at the point of attack. Since the defense must handle both sides of the formation, creating inside running paths is easier.

2. The Double Wing Offense

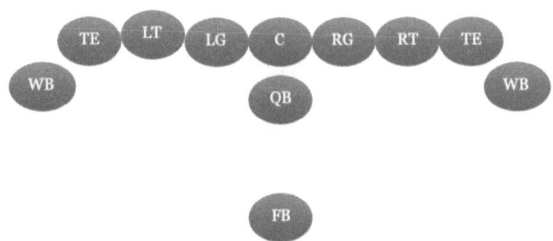

The double wing offense is another popular form of youth football. Like the I formation, this formation features five line players: two tight ends, two guards, and a center. Aligned perpendicular with the offensive line is the quarterback and fullback. Two wing backs occupy the two sides of the formation.

The purpose of the double wing offense formation is to double-team a block and pierce open more defense holes for the ball carrier. Most importantly, you can implement this formation to execute various plays, such as the power run, counterplay, or power passing play.

Some of the benefits of this formation are that it's easy to install, supports multiple plays, easy to implement, difficult to defend against, unpredictable for the defense, and offers more ball carrier options. However, this formation is only ideal if you have a fast, running quarterback and players who can pull.

3. The Wishbone Formation

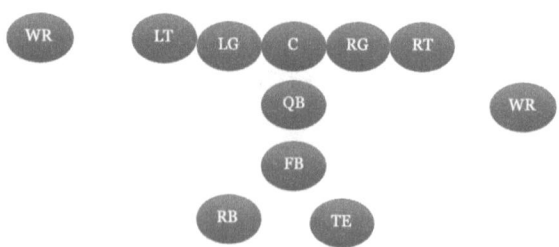

The wishbone formation is a power running offense scheme popular in youth football. It features two tight ends, one fullback, two halfbacks, a center, two guards, and two tackles. The quarterback takes the spot just behind the center.

Like the double wing offense, the wishbone formation double teams at the point of attack. The three backfield players allow the offensive players to play the double team on a targeted defense player. Halfbacks lead the block on some plays. Tight ends can be great catchers, posing threats to the defense. Sometimes, they widen the field and execute a block for the running back to run with the ball. The main benefits of the wishbone formation include the following:

- It's a power running formation, which can be suitable for youth football players.
- Offers multiple blocking chances for offensive line players.
- The defense will likely lose the ball when three running backs go in different directions, making this formation ideal for a counter game.
- It sets up opportunities for play action pass plays due to its high success in running the ball.
- It can be used to confuse the defense and create scoring opportunities.

- It's easy to implement and has proven successful in youth football.

4. *The Single Wing Offense*

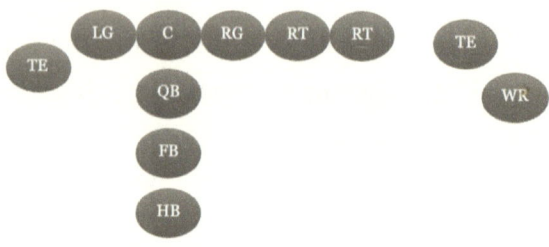

The single wing formation is an unbalanced offense scheme that can cause defense confusion if well planned. This formation features the tight end split away to the far side, followed by the left guard, center, right guard, and double tackles. Unlike in other formations, the quarterback is positioned not behind the center but at the tackle position.

On the left behind the quarterback, slightly split from the inner foot of the quarterback, is a fullback, then a tailback in the backfield away from the fullback. The backbone of this formation's success is its unbalanced formation. This keeps the defense off balance, causing them headaches since many youth football teams run balanced formations.

The main objective of the single wing back formation is to double-team at the point of attack. This is how to get the extra blocker:

- There are two tackles on one side of the center, leaving the other side with the tight end and one guard.
- The positioning of the wing back allows them to rush into the blocking position. You should have a strong, quick, and vigilant player in this position.
- The fullback and quarterback will block for the ball carrier at some point in the game, creating running lanes.

You don't need to field a traditional quarterback using this offensive scheme. If you include them, they can block and run with the ball. Some of the benefits of this formation include the following:

- Easy installation, making it ideal for practicing in the first week of the season
- Great at deceiving the defense and keeping it off balance
- Has some good play-action passing plays, and the quarterback

- It's difficult to stop the wedge play at the youth football level

5. *The Split Back Formation*

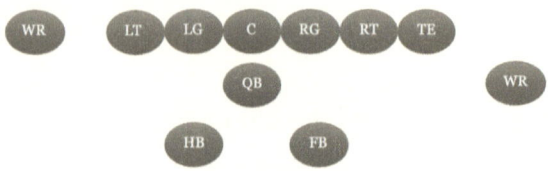

The split back formation, also known as the pro set, is an offense that gained popularity in the National Football League many years back. It has become uncommon in modern football. However, it's still a popular offense scheme in youth football because it's effective.

The split back offense consists of five line players, one slot back, a split end, and two split halfbacks. You can run various plays with this formation, including power, counter play, sweep, and trap plays.

This formation provides a lot of options to run your offense. Its strength is that you can go unbalanced and confuse your opponent's defense. For example, you can opt to play with one or two receivers. Slot backs, often fast, can be used as ball receivers, catchers, and run with the ball.

If you have the players with the right skill sets, you can't go wrong with this formation. The base of well formation execution is practice.

6. The T Formation

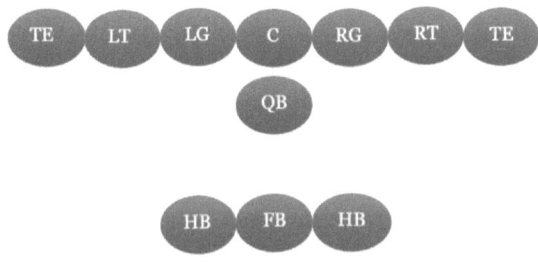

When most of your players are new to the offense, the T formation can be a great offensive scheme. The reason is that it teaches how to play a football game while it confuses the defense. The T formation focuses more on running the ball than passing it.

It positions five offensive line players at the line of scrimmage made up of two tackles, two guards, and a center. Two tight ends occupy positions on either side of the center while the quarterback slots behind the center. In the backfield, you line up two halfbacks and a fullback.

The center, quarterback, and fullback align in a straight line perpendicular to the offensive line. The two halfbacks each slot in line with the left and right guards.

When viewed from the line of scrimmage, this scheme forms the letter T with the running backs aligned horizontally.

The T formation is balanced with many variations, making it hard to predict the next move. Not only is the T formation easy to teach and implement, but it is also difficult for the defense to identify who will get the ball in the next play. Give this formation a go if you have children with little football experience, a mobile quarterback, and great running backs.

7. The Spread Offense

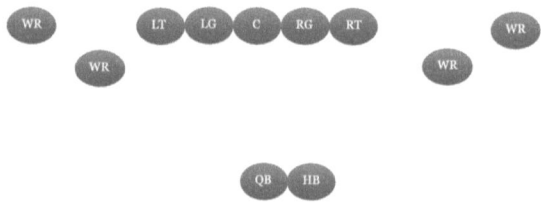

The spread offense has become common in modern football. You primarily use this offense scheme to stretch the defense by widening the field. As the defense spreads horizontally across the field, it leaves some inside holes that the quarterback or running back can exploit. That's why it's a great formation to employ when you have an athletic quarterback.

One variation of the spread offense features a center, two guards, and two tackles on the offensive line. On both sides of the offensive line, you field double receivers. The quarterback sits a few yards behind the center, closes by, and you position the running back.

Placing the quarterback in shotgun will allow them to see easier and release the ball to the athletic player quickly.

8. The Wing T Offense

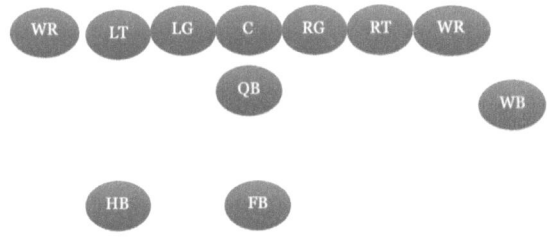

The Wing T offense is also one of the best football formations for youth. This formation boasts five offensive line players, two wing backs, one tight end, one split-end, a quarterback, and a fullback. It is an unpredictable formation.

The cause of the defense's uncertainty stems from the split-ends inclusion. You want to play something other than predictable youth football, which is one reason to use the wing T formation. The reason is that it uses multiple players going in different directions and confuses the defense. Amid this confusion, passing play lanes become available and can encourage good passages of play.

The wing T formation can be implemented to run various plays, including reverses, short passing plays, counters, and bootlegs. This formation is ideal for you if you have the following:

- Players who can't play a power running game but can run the ball smoothly
- A quarterback who's adept at throwing the ball and can run
- Speedy backfield players who're good ball carriers

You cannot successfully implement this formation if you have running backs who can't block and offensive line players who can't run fast.

As stated earlier, you should know your players before choosing an offensive formation. Don't only consider players' speed, but check their body sizes, strengths, and weaknesses. You can understand why I can't recommend a particular formation. You'll know when you found the right one because it'll work for your team.

HOW TO COACH DEFENSE

You can't win games if you concede more points than you score. It's the purpose of defense to stop the opponents from scoring against you. This makes this chapter crucial as you build your youth football team.

TEACH THESE SIX FUNDAMENTALS OF YOUTH FOOTBALL DEFENSE

There are few fundamentals of effective defense in football. The six main fundamentals of youth football defense are tackling, alignment, defensive stance, rushing the passer, covering the receiver, pursuing the ball, creating turnovers, and defeating blockers. If you get all of them right, your team will be hard to stop.

1. Tackling

Good tackling is critical for youth football team success. Of more importance is ensuring that your players practice safe tackling, which I previously suggested—the shoulder tackling technique. I've already detailed how this technique works. Consider revisiting it before you practice it.

Your players should be able to execute angle and open field tackling because it's essential for your team's performance. Get your team to practice this tackling as often as possible, if not daily.

2. Alignment

The second fundamental of good defense is proper alignment. Most importantly, you can't have a rigid defense formation; it must be flexible to counter the offense's formation. You can implement two defensive alignments: man-to-man defense and zone defense.

Man-to-man defense: In this alignment, you assign each defensive player to cover a specific offensive player. It works well, provided you have speedy defensive players. It is essential to take a closer look at the different types of defensive alignments to see how your choice of coverage can affect the game. Consider your opponents and their current performance before deciding on this defensive alignment.

Zone defense: This is an alternative defense alignment in which you assign a defensive player to cover a specific zone of the field. Zone defense is helpful to defend against huge plays since help is usually close by. The main drawback of zone defense is that the opponent may overload an area of the field. There's a way to counter this: Cover the deepest offensive player unless the opponent throws the ball to a different offensive player.

3. Defensive Stance

Every defensive player should set up their body correctly right off the bat so they can react swiftly. Linebackers and defensive backs need to assume proper stances to have an impact in their respective positions.

The defensive line players should assume the three-point stance. Some players might be uncomfortable with this stance, preferring the four-point stance. That's fine. The key is that the defensive line's stance should be a bit wider than that of the offensive line to achieve better balance. Their bodies need to be low for powerful take-offs.

Linebackers should have their feet shoulder-width apart and slightly staggered. They also should bend their knees slightly to assume low body positions. Their eyes should be directed to the player from whom they'll receive a cue. Linebackers must stand somewhat upright with their shoulders in front of their hips. You can refer to the defense drills we covered earlier for more details.

Irrespective of the defensive alignment, defensive backs and linebackers must move swiftly as soon as the center snaps the ball. This quick reaction will help counter any advantage the offense has, such as knowing when their desired play will begin.

4. Rushing the Passer

When play begins, the offensive players often block aggressively. In contrast, they sit back when they intend to pass the ball. Your defensive line players must be able to spot this change in approach and immediately put pressure on the QB. At this point, your defensive players must identify which offensive player will block them. This is the player to defeat before they hunt for the QB.

For the defensive line players to be effective with pass rushes, they need to know where the QB will set up. Your task as a coach is to charge them with planning their pass-rush approach every time a play starts. Armed with this plan, your defensive players will have a greater chance of overcoming the pass protection block and reaching the QB.

There are three ways your defensive players can rush the QB: the rip or swim technique, the spin technique, or the bull rush technique. Let's briefly look at what each of these techniques is about and how it works.

The rip or swim technique: The defensive player swiftly goes around the offensive player and attacks the QB. The defensive player repositions the blocker by using the arm furthest from the block while the other arm opens up space for the defensive player to pass the blocker. The defensive player needs to start this technique when close to the blocker, or else it won't work.

The spin technique: The defensive players use arms and hands to spin the blocker and reach the offensive backfield. To be effective with this technique, a defender gets closer to the offensive lineman and hits them in the chest. Next, with the forearm on the side of the spin before throwing the opposite arm around, the defender simultaneously pushes off the blocker with the forearm. To execute this technique successfully, the defensive player must be close to the blocker.

The bull rush technique: The bull rush strategy happens when the defensive player locks both arms off and into the armpits of the offensive blocker, lifts them, and forces them into the QB. This technique is ideal for defensive players with good arm and hand strength.

5. Covering the Receiver

When defending, you'll have two groups of defensive players: One group rushes the QB as they set up to throw the ball, and the second group attempts to stop the offense from catching the ball if the QB throws it. If the QB makes a successful pass to a receiver, the defense must tackle them immediately. This second group of defensive players, which often includes linebackers and defensive backs, are said to take part in pass coverage.

To effectively cover the receivers, the defensive players must align adequately, backpedal, and execute the appropriate pass coverage strategy.

Proper alignment: To align properly, the defensive corners line up 5–7 yards from the receivers while the safeties line up 8–12 yards deep off the slot receiver or tight end. If you place one safely, get them to line up deep in the middle of the field. This setup allows the defensive corners and safeties to make plays whether the offense passes or runs the ball.

Backpedal: The first step for the defensive backs is to move away from the line of scrimmage as soon as an offensive play begins. This movement allows them to establish whether the offense runs or passes the ball. The backpedal move starts with a push off the front foot and a step backward with the back foot. For the defensive backs to be ready when receivers break to catch the ball, they should stay in control. They achieve this as follows:

- Bend their waist forward, then reach back with each step and pull their body over their feet
- Relaxing arms and keeping them in running style
- Maintain their shoulders in front of their hips

Pass coverage: There are two basic types of pass coverage: man-to-man coverage and zone coverage. Whether you favor man-to-man pass coverage or zone pass coverage, you must drill your defense on pass coverage. In zone pass coverage, a defensive player moves into a selected area of the field to deflect or catch any pass thrown into that zone. The focus of defensive players is on the QB. In man-to-man coverage, each defender focuses on a specific receiver's belt region, stays, and tracks them throughout an offensive play. This type of coverage requires mental toughness, agility, and speed.

6. Pursuit to the Football

Once the offense has the ball in the hands of the ball carrier, your defense must get to them as fast as possible. Taking the right angle to the ball for faster tackling is vital. A defense that gets to the ball carrier rarely gives up big plays and improves the team's chances of winning games.

Swarming the ball with passion and energy is a trademark of top defense. This is achieved through gang tackling, securing gaps, and getting to pursuit lanes.

7. Creating Turnovers

Creating turnovers can be the difference between losing and winning. When your team wins turnovers, the opposing team gets demoralized. This adds energy and positivity to your team. This is where swarming to the ball can come in handy.

When intending to create turnovers, the main priority is first to secure the tackle. With gang tackling, your defense players can hack at the ball, which often results in turnovers. It would be best if you practiced swarming to the ball, gang tackling, and hacking at the ball as much as possible during training.

Another aspect of creating turnovers is getting an interception. It can be hard to create interceptions in youth football because most youth football focuses on running plays. Even then, if you keep wide receivers in front of you and deliver big blows, the ball will often pop out, resulting in an interception. In addition, an ill-advised pass by the quarterback is another massive opportunity for an interception.

8. Defeating Blockers

Every football coach and player knows the importance of the QB. However, the QB can only be successful if offensive blockers play their part. Defensive players should understand that they should defeat the offensive blocker before identifying the ball carrier and partici-pating in the tackle.

Your defense can spot whether the offense will run the ball or not. Typically, the offensive line players immedi-ately attack across the line of scrimmage as soon as the center snaps the balls. Immediately, the defense should figure out who will be the blocker to stand a chance of attacking the QB faster. Often, the offensive blocker will be close and directly in front of the defense line players or on one side. Defensive backs can spot quickly which offensive player is assigned to block them.

Immediately the blocker is identified, the defensive players must step into them. Importantly the blocker's pads should be above during the attack. If a defensive line player meets the blocker, they should raise their forearm into the blocker's body while simultaneously making contact with the blocker with shoulder pads. This should stop the momentum of the blocker and make it easier for the defense to push them away and locate the ball carrier.

Note that your defense can only make tackles once they've defeated the blocker. With this in mind, get your team to practice rip moves.

KEYS TO COACHING THE DEFENSIVE LINE

youth football coaches sometimes pay little attention to defensive line plays. Your defensive line can help you win the line of scrimmage and control games. When you dictate games, you'll win many games. Winning the line of scrimmage requires you to have a strong and technically prepared defensive line. This is where the following techniques and responsibilities should be part of your daily practice.

Attacking on Ball Movement

Your defenders must be ready to go on the offense as soon as the ball moves. Every defensive line coach should ensure that the defensive linemen watch the ball all the time! As soon as the ball moves, the defensive line must take off and not wait for the QB's cue. Opponents may try to make your defenders jump off-sides on hard counts or fast counts.

Sometimes the offense can shift formations to get your defensive line to jump off-sides. Ignore this and get your team to focus on ball movement. It's a good idea to drill your defense to move only on ball movement. For example, you can start all drills when the ball moves.

Staying Low-Launching

When your defensive line players launch low, they make it difficult for the offensive line players to push them around. Your defenders should launch into the blocker immediately after the ball is snapped.

A vital coaching point is that the defensive line players should attempt to rip through the block. This is because running around the block will take them out of play, offering the offense a chance to run with the ball. Additionally, running around the block makes the defensive line players leave their gap unmanned. Get them off with active feet and hands inside and rip through the block.

Squeezing

One quality of good defense is squeezing the offensive line players. Yet this skill will cut off cutback lanes, any space, and voided gaps. Surprisingly, many youth football coaches need to teach this skill.

Squeezing is when a defensive player presses down onto an offensive line player who pulls or down blocks away from them.

Teach your defensive line players that if they're not getting blocked, they're being trapped or kicked out by the opponent's offensive line player or a running back. The antidote to this offensive approach is to squeeze down and take on the kick or trap block to counter the play.

Unless you implement squeezing, single and double wing schemes will destroy your team. Teach your defensive line players how to squeeze and do it effectively.

Block Shedding

Also called block destruction, block shedding is crucial for defensive line players. This technique allows the defensive line to shed blockers and charge for the ball carrier.

There are two standard methods for block shedding in youth football: the swim move and the rip move. I've introduced you to these techniques earlier. The best approach for block shedding is the rip move. It forces the defender to stay low during contact with the blocker. Immediately contact with the blocker occurs, the defensive line player rips their inside arm and drives through them. Your team will only tackle the ball carrier if it can be effective at block destruction.

Gaps Assignments

Manning gaps during defending is as crucial as making tackles. Every member of the defensive line should be assigned a gap to defend and attack. Every technique that the offense or defense employs aims at plugging the gap at the line of scrimmage.

In football, the defensive gaps are designated letters A, B, C, and D, irrespective of the side of the field you're considering. Here's the meaning of these gaps.

- **A-gap:** The space between the offensive guard and center
- **B-gap:** The space between the offensive tackle and the offensive guard
- **C-gap:** The space between the tight end and the offensive tackle
- **D-gap:** The spaces on the outside shoulders of the tight ends

Defenders must secure their gap because the offense can hit you with counterplays, often running plays.

Anchoring Gaps

Every football coach dreams of a defensive line that swarms the ball carrier. This will likely happen if the defense line players anchor their assigned gaps. The eagerness to chase opens up the defense for big offensive plays.

The defense must chase but do so at the right time. It's better to first penetrate and anchor the gap before pursuing the ball carrier.

WHAT TO DO BEFORE DRAWING UP THE DEFENSE

Where do you begin when drawing your defense? It all starts with the kind of players you have. A list of players you have, active or inactive, is called a roster. The roster holds important information about each player, including their weight, height, and jersey number. You'll use it throughout the season.

Armed with a roster, divide your defensive team into three categories: defensive line, defensive back, and linebacker. Avoid categorizing players exclusively on their weight or height. Plenty of big children can begin to play from a two-point stance.

Your roster will also guide you on what defense system to play. For example, if you have many linebacker types of players, a 4-4 defense may be your best option.

TOP SIX DEFENSIVE FORMATIONS

Playing sound defense puts your team in an excellent position to win games and ensures players are safe. You don't have to learn all available defense plays since there are only about six primary defense plays. There are variations, but those will be easy to understand once you've internalized the basic formations. Let's go over each of these six basic youth defense plays.

1. The 5-3 Youth Football Defense

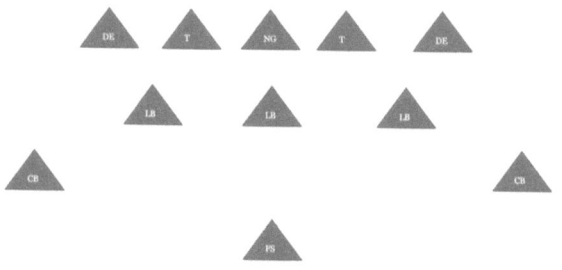

There is no rule in youth football that says you must run an even front defensive line. The 5-3 defense play employs eight defenders at the line of scrimmage. What's different is that the front consists of a nose guard, two tackles, and two ends, making it an excellent play for teams having only five or six defensive line players. Who can tell when one of your defensive line players will miss a game or two for some reason?

This kind of play is sound when you have a talented nose guard. The reason is that it positions your best players as close to the ball as possible. With the 5-3 defense play, the nose guard can obstruct the offensive team's blocking strategy to allow swarming of the ball.

As I've already mentioned, destroying the block is key in defense. The 5-3 football defense is suited for this because it can slant in one way or another. This slant is made possible by the 5-3 defense's perfect balance on the snap.

2. The 4-4 Youth Football Defense

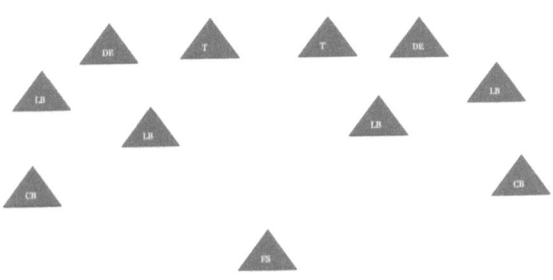

The 4-4 youth football defense positions eight players close to the line of scrimmage. It consists of four linemen and four linebackers, making it a sound formation when you have more linebacker types of players on your roster. In this defense, the secondary features two cornerbacks, a strong safety, and a free safety

Using this defense, you can confuse the offense's blocking scheme and improve your chances of a blitz. It's also a tremendous run-stopping defense like a defense play called the 6-2 defense, which I'll talk about shortly.

The 4-4 defense can be adjusted to defend against teams that spread the field. For example, you can cover the slot receivers and still defend the run. Additionally, you can adjust the 4-4 youth football defense to receiver motions. Your four linebackers need to understand run flow either toward or away from them.

3. The 4-3 Youth Football Defense

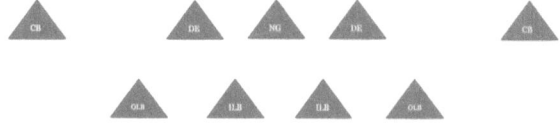

The 4-3 youth football defense allows you to employ players in different positions. That and its easy implementation are reasons why it's so common among professional teams and numerous youth teams. It features four linemen, two outside linebackers, and one middle linebacker. You might hear the three linebackers referred to as Sam, Mike, and Will. Behind these players, you have two cornerbacks and a free and strong safety in the secondary.

There are variations of the 4-3 defense, but the basic goal is gap control. The 4-3 defense is designed to counter passes because the cover two works well in passing situations.

4. The 3-3 Stack Youth Football Defense

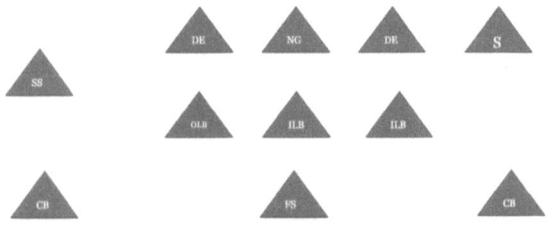

The 3-3 stack youth football defense is effective for gap control defense. It's great for countering the modern spread offenses while remaining effective run-heavy offenses. Its simplicity allows players to focus on mastery since few skill sets are required.

The 3-3 stack defense consists of two middle linebackers, one linebacker stacked over the center, and two outside linebackers: the secondary features two cornerbacks and a free safety or deep middle safety.

The nose guard and the linebacker behind them man the A-gaps while the tackles look after the B-gaps. It's crucial that the two middle linebackers rip through the offense, or they'll be pushed off and disrupt the effectiveness of the defense.

5. The 5-2 Youth Football Defense

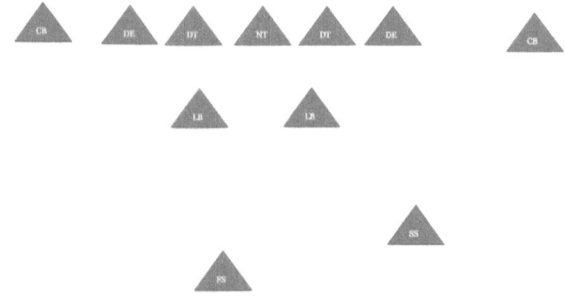

The defense formations we've dealt with primarily focused on stopping the run. What if you face an opponent with a QB who can change the game with their throws? Unless you have a way to counter that sort of offensive play, you'll have many unhappy weekends. This is where you can employ the 5-2 youth football defense.

This system features two inside linebackers with two cornerbacks. It also includes weak and strong safety, making this system a powerful defense play. The reason is that strong safety allows the team to adjust quickly to multiple offensive plays by just moving one player. The strong safety can play against slants, screens, and flare passes.

6. The 6-2 Youth Football Defense

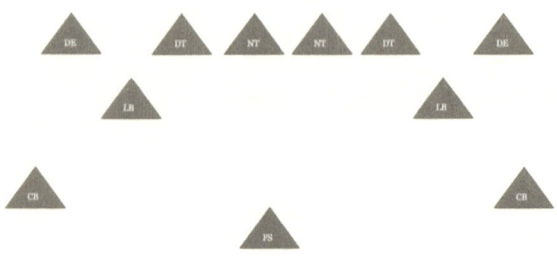

The 6-2 defense is the best defense against runs at the youth football level. The reason is that fewer QBs can hurt you with throws at this level than at higher levels like high school or college. Furthermore, it's a simple defense play. If you want an ideal defense for offensive isolation runs and power plays, the 6-2 defense is your go-to system.

This formation consists of six down line players, two inside linebackers, two cornerbacks, and a safety. Each player is responsible for manning a particular gap, making it essential to teach gap assignments before the center snaps the ball. Sometimes it's hard to find youth football linebackers which you can overcome by putting your two best players as inside linebackers. Since it gives up significant yardage, the 6-2 defense can hide some of your minimum-play players in the line's interior. Remember that the focus of this defense is to stop runs.

8

HOW TO COACH SPECIAL TEAMS

Special teams are one of the three main phases of football. One of the mistakes that a youth football coach can make is to overlook special teams. Doing this can cost your team extra points, field goals, and opportunities created by punts and kickoffs. Some defensive and offensive team players might slip up on their roles as special teams players. It's your role to remind them of the importance of special teams. In this chapter, we'll look at how you can coach special teams and reap the benefits they bring to a football team.

THE KICKOFF TEAM

The kickoff team takes the field at the beginning of the game, after you've scored, or at the start of the second half. The kicker's responsibility is to kick the ball downfield. The role of the rest of the kickoff team players is to run down the field as the kicker kicks the ball. Their goal is to position themselves to tackle the defending team's kick returner, who wants to run the ball back up the field. Before we go over how the kicker can be effective in your youth football team, let's cover some basics about kickoffs.

We can now dive into how the kicker does their job effectively. A kickoff is when the kicker kicks the ball to the opposing team down the field. A legal kickoff must go at least 10 yards down the field or be touched by the opposing team.

The Kicker

The kicker must build sufficient momentum to kick the football as far into the opposing team's side as possible. Here's how they get this right.

- They place the ball on the tee placed behind the restraining line. The receiving team's restraining line is 10 yards ahead of the kicking team.

- The kicker lines up, so the kicking foot is positioned directly behind the ball and the tee while the other foot stands to the side of the tee.
- In a straight line, the kicker turns and takes about eight steps from the football.
- Then, they turn and ensure they're still in line with the ball. If not in line, they adjust to the left or right to be in line with the ball.
- The kicker turns and takes five steps to the left if they're right-footed. Otherwise, they take the five steps to the right. They should now be about nine-and-a-half steps from the ball.
- They turn to face the ball and take a short forward step with the kicking foot.
- The kicker now begins their forward run to the ball by moving the kicking foot first.
- They then begin to build momentum as they approach the ball slowly.
- The kicker positions the non-kicking foot about four inches and six inches behind and outside the ball, respectively. They should ensure this foot points straight down the field.
- Keeping their shoulders forward, eyes on the ball, and the kicking leg behind their body, the kicker hits the ball at about four inches from the bottom of the ball. Placing the kicking leg

behind the ball allows the kicker to swing the kicking foot in an arch as it approaches the ball.

- As they kick the ball, they keep their head down and follow through with the kicking leg smoothly.
- After kicking the ball, the kicker becomes safe and positions themselves in front of the returner's route.

The Team

Let's now focus on what the remainder of the kickoff team does. Important points to emphasize when coaching youth football about effective kickoff team plays. The aim should be to force the kickoff returner into running to the inside of the field. This is achieved by getting the kickoff team's two outside players to run down closer to the sidelines.

- Tell your players to start 10 yards behind the ball to stay onside during kickoff.
- Each player must run down the field in their lane.
- As the players near the ball carrier, they should shorten their strides to maintain control and position themselves to make the tackle.
- Every player must be in line with the rest of the kickoff team as they run down the field.

Like with all football plays, it's necessary to drill your players on kickoff plays so that they execute them without overthinking.

THE KICKOFF RETURN

When the opponent executes a kickoff, your special team should be able to catch the ball and return it. A player who catches and returns the ball following a kickoff play is known as a kickoff returner. The kickoff return should be able to catch the ball and run up the field until they're tackled, score a touchdown, or forced out of the field. Since scoring touchdowns is rare in return plays, the main aim of the kickoff returner is to gain yardage up the field. The rest of the players block for the kickoff return once the ball has been kicked.

For your kickoff returns to work, place two players on each side of the field. Players need to line up to see the kicker before the snap. When the ball is kicked, one of the return players should call out to their partner, "I have it. I have it." Immediately, the partner positions themselves to block.

Having good technique is crucial for kick returners. For example, the returner making the catch should do this:

- Position themselves in front of the flight of the football.
- Place the little fingers of both hands together as they reach up, which allows them to see both their hands and the ball as it comes down.
- Catch and bring the ball to their body to secure it as they return to the identified area of the football field.
- Most importantly, run the ball up the field as far as possible before being tackled.

Assigning each kickoff return player an opponent to block during a kick return is a good idea. Immediately after the kicking team kicks the ball, blockers should line up between the area where the returner will run and their assigned offensive player. The remaining players on the kickoff team block the opposing team to make the return successful.

This avoids blocking the kickoff coverage too early. The reason is that there's still too much space for the offensive players to run around your blockers. Once the ball is kicked, your blockers should form a wall around the kickoff returner, blocking downfield. Your players shouldn't lock arms or stand shoulder to shoulder as this is considered a wedge, which isn't allowed in many youth leagues.

One of the mistakes that blockers make is to leave their feet and dive when making blocks. This needs to be more effective. Instead, blockers should target the offensive players' front jersey numbers and execute the block.

THE PUNT TEAM

The main aim of the punt team is to ensure that the offensive team starts as close to their end zone as possible. If your team gets the punt wrong, it may be blocked and lead to a potential high-scoring chance for your opponents. This is why the punter kicks deep, there's a telepathic and clean long snapper/punter exchange, and you limit the opponent's punt return.

When coaching punters, there's nothing as important as teaching the correct techniques. There needs to be more because players must practice the techniques to execute them with minimal thinking. Only then will your punt team improve the consistency and distance of its punts.

The punt team is the special teams unit you'll use most often during a game. The reason is that most teams usually punt on fourth down. There are two main players on the punt team: the long snapper and the punter. The long snapper, also called the center, snaps the ball back through their legs to the punter, who can stand about 10–15 yards from them. The punter catches the ball and punts it as far as possible in the opponent's territory.

Like in the kickoff team, the rest players serve as blockers to protect the punter until they successfully kick the ball. The opponent often catches the punt and attempts to return it up the field. The blockers tackle the opposing team's players and try to bring them down before advancing the ball up the field. Keeping the ball in the air for as long as possible gives the blockers time to run down the field and tackle the ball carrier.

Sometimes the punter needs more time to kick the ball. This is where your blockers must block the opposing players first to allow the punter to kick the ball before they run down the field.

Let's now look at the techniques for effective punting by both the long snapper and the punter.

The Long Snapper

There are two critical techniques long snappers use to be effective: the method of handling the ball and how they start. Most long snappers place their feet even when they begin the snaps. They hold the ball as if throwing a forward pass with their snapping hand. The non-throwing hand is placed on the top of the ball to guide for a better position during the snap.

The following necessary setup is the stance. Long snappers stand so that the shoulders are even, their back level, and the height of the rear and shoulders are the same.

When the punter is ready, long snappers aim to hit the punter's belt with the ball. During the snap, their hands rotate the ball to the outside.

A long snap can go above the punter's head because their back needs to be level. Drill your long snappers on keeping their back level when long snapping.

The Punter

The punter aims to kick the ball as far to the opponent's part of the field as possible. These guidelines will help your punters do their job effectively:

- They should position themselves 10 yards from the long snapper.
- Stand with the non-kicking foot slightly back and hands in front of the belt. The front number should be fully visible.
- Catch the ball, take a short forward step with the kicking foot, and simultaneously extend the ball forward.

- Take a normal step with the non-kicking foot and move the hand opposite the kicking foot away from the ball.
- Kick the ball at its center and follow through with the kicking leg. Meanwhile, the non-kicking foot should be grounded when kicking the ball.

The rest of the punt team blocks your opponent's punt rushers to allow for a successful punt. Proper alignment is crucial for punt blocking, which should often be foot-to-foot split and low stances for leverage.

Once the ball is kicked, the punter yells 'go' for the team to stop blocking. The punter also gives the direction of the ball. It's, therefore, essential to coach your punter on yelling the direction of the punt and directing the punt. It would be best if you drilled your team on long snapping and kicking every practice day.

Punt Coverage Drill

The punt team's job is done once they've covered the punt. Here's how to drill your punt team on punt coverage.

- Line up a guard, tackle, and tight end on either side of the center.

- Have each defensive line player secure the inside gap. The center should secure the A-gap, as do the guards.
- Place one wing back on either side of the center to secure the D-gap.
- The holder should become the wide safety after the punt is successful, while the punter becomes a safety.
- Start the whistle to kick off the punt.
- The special team should first block on the inside to allow a successful punt.
- As soon as the punt is kicked, the special team should fan out to cover the returner on the outside.

Ensure that your team practices punting and long snapping daily.

THE PUNT RETURN TEAM

The punt return team operates similarly to the kickoff return team. The punt team aims to catch a punt and return it as far up the field as possible. The punt returner must be able to catch the ball and run up the field with it. The player making the catch should do what I recommended the kickoff returner does.

The punt returner has three options for catching the punt: They can stop or catch the ball after raising one arm above their head and motioning it back and forth —a play called a fair catch, catch the punt, or allow the ball to hit the ground. After a fair catch, the punt returner isn't allowed to run with the ball, and the opposition can't tackle them either.

Your players should run to their designated blocking positions on the field as soon as the ball is punted. Coach your special teams to ensure they contain players and don't run into the kicker.

THE EXTRA POINT KICK

The extra point kick is an opportunity for the team that scored a touchdown to score an additional point. Scoring an extra point may occur by kicking the ball through the goalposts and over the crossbar, passing, or running the ball. After a successful kick in youth football, two points are added to the scoreboard.

Three players who use special techniques in this situation are the kicker, holder, and short snapper or the center. The rest of the players block for the kicker to successfully kick the ball through the uprights of the goalposts.

The Kicker

Kickers can use two basic placekicks: soccer and straight-ahead styles. There's no need to stress, which is effective because both work well. Here are the steps the kicker should follow to make successful kicks.

- Position themselves three steps behind the location of the kick. If using the soccer style, they should then move two steps to the side.
- With eyes on the kicking spot, the kicker should place the kicking foot behind the other.
- Move the non-kicking foot a short step forward and then take a longer-than-usual step with the kicking foot.
- Position the non-kicking leg about their shoe's length from and to the side of the ball. They should ensure that the non-kicking foot points at the middle of the goalposts.
- The kicker's kicking leg should be bent behind the body and swung smoothly.
- Hit the ball with the large bone on top of the foot and about four inches above the tee.
- Follow through the kick and finish when the kicking leg is opposite the non-kicking leg side's shoulder.

The Holder

The holder's role is to catch the snap from the center and place it on a kicking tee. As soon as the holder has placed the tee on the ground, they should position themselves to catch the ball from the short snapper. The following helps the holder to perform their function:

- They should kneel on the ground with their back knee while the front leg is up and points at the center of the goalposts.
- The holder checks for the reach to the tee by reaching down with their backhand.
- They ensure that the kicker is ready to kick the ball.
- The holder creates a target for the short snapper by placing the thumbs and little fingers of their right and left hands together.
- They receive the snap and balance the ball at the top with the index finger of the backhand.
- Then, they gently spin the ball with the other hand to bring the ball's laces to the front.

The Short Snapper

The Short snapper positions themselves relative to the holder the same way as the long snapper. The difference is that the target for the short snapper is below that of the punter. As soon as the snap is completed, the short snapper should help with the block, which brings us to how blocking should take place.

Blocking for the Extra Point Kick

The remaining players on the extra point kicking team block the opponent to ensure a successful kick. When the long snapper snaps the ball, the block should target the inside gaps. For blocking to be effective, ensure your players do the following:

- Each line player should step back with the inside foot to lean inside and gain leverage and power.
- Your line players should stay low while blocking backs assume wide bases.
- The team blocks anyone who comes inside.

The snap count should be fast to prevent the defense from blocking the kick. Otherwise, you may opt for the hard count to induce the defense into jumping offsides.

THE EXTRA POINT BLOCK

Extra points can make a big difference between winning and losing games. The team that blocks extra points successfully can win tight games. That's why you shouldn't only practice converting extra points and blocking extra points from being scored against you during each practice. To do this, you need to have a blocking scheme you understand.

Two powerful extra-point block schemes are the overload blitz and the twist blitz. Both of these schemes can be implemented to the right or left.

Overload Blitz Left Side

An overload blitz on the left side packs more defenders on the left of the center than the offense can match. There's a defensive line player who covers each offensive line player. Additionally, linebackers man the gaps between each pair of defensive line players.

The defensive line players cover the offensive line players' blocks and bull-rush them backward. This will give the blitzing linebackers a lane to charge at the extra point kick attempt. For this to work, have the best athletes as your blitzing linebackers. Remember, you can overload the right side if circumstances allow.

Twist Right Side

The other option to blitz the extra point kick attempt is to run a twist on the right side. Like in the overload on the left side, the defensive line players each line up against an offensive line player. Instead of bull-rushing them, they'll rip through their outside shoulders.

In this play, the middle linebacker lines up behind the right tackle. Once the short snapper snaps the ball, they blitz the A-gap.

9

COACHING ON GAME DAY

You've drilled your youth football team on various skills and techniques required for effective defense and offense. Today is GAME DAY! Parents, friends of your players, fans, and the team anticipate winning the game. This is the day to execute the plan you've been working on with players and assistant coaches. You now primarily switch from teaching to coaching. However, the game is a significant teacher, and you cannot afford to turn a blind eye to that fact, although the focus is on winning.

Execution should cover three periods critical to winning games: before, during, and after the game. This chapter will guide you, so you're prepared for every game.

THE NIGHT BEFORE THE GAME

Few things in youth football beat the importance of diet and nutrition. Players must have stamina and energy to execute well-orchestrated plays you designed and successfully tested in practice. The night before the game, your players should have a proper diet.

Protein is crucial for building your players' muscles. The diet should include lean protein from fish, chicken, or turkey. Additionally, they should ingest healthy carbohydrates such as whole wheat pasta, whole grain bread, sweet potatoes, or brown rice. Healthy carbohydrates supply needed fuel and energy for growth.

To have a balanced diet, encourage your players to include fresh and leafy green vegetables. Most importantly, they should hydrate as much as possible. The bulk of their bodies is water, and players can only function optimally when there's enough of it in the body. Get your players to sleep early to have sufficient rest to prevent fatigue the following day.

Encourage your players to eat food they're familiar with the night before and before the game. Otherwise, they might suffer gastrointestinal issues and be unavailable for games.

The second important thing is that players should pack their game gear the night before. This ensures that they remember crucial clothing or equipment.

PREGAME PREPARATIONS

There are some essential preparations needed before the game can start. Your players should have a pregame meal and have the proper clothing and equipment. Let's first look at what they should eat before the game.

The purpose of the pregame meal is to provide fuel, store enough carbohydrates, and supply sufficient energy to the brain. Like the meal the night before the game, your players should ingest quick-digesting food such as carbohydrates and proteins. Fats are a no-go because they digest slowly. Good pregame carbohydrates include bran and rice, while protein sources such as skinless chicken and low-fat yogurt are great choices. I discourage using replacement meals and sports beverages as replacements for the pregame meal. If a player wants a large meal, they should consume it at least three to four hours before the start of the game.

It's unforgivable to forget that players must have their team uniform to play the game. You should ensure that they have all equipment, such as mouth guards, knee pads, shoes, and thigh pads. Clothing should be worn before players enter the field.

You should have a rule on the arrival time of the game. Whatever the time, you and your assistant coaches should arrive at least an hour before the start of the game. Timely arrival allows your team to have enough time to warm up. Set a rule that says players should arrive at the game at least 45 minutes before the game commences.

CHECKLIST BEFORE KICK OFF

Checklists ensure that we don't give our memories chances of forgetting what's important. Pilots use checklists to ensure planes are safe to fly, so you should provide every facet of the game goes according to plan. Some of the actions you want to include in your check-list are:

- The name of the field commissioner
- Objectives for your offense, defense, and special teams
- Phone numbers of players and their parents. You may have to call them because the player is late.
- The name of the opponent's head coach
- Names of the referees

Think carefully about what to include in your checklists. They must be items crucial for winning the game.

UNPLANNED EVENTS

Planning and being organized don't mean that things will proceed according to the plan. Some things can be anticipated and planned for, while others are difficult. There are times when unexpected events may occur. For example, the game might be called off due to unforeseen circumstances such as rain or crime at the venue. Other negative things that could impact your game plan include players coming late or not showing up.

Eventualities such as an injury to a key player or an unavailable player can be prepared for. The same applies if you can't be available due to an emergency or you'll be late. As a result, these unforeseen circumstances must be part of your game plan.

You can't do much about a game postponed, but you can inform parents well in time if the game is called off the day before it starts. Encourage your players to come to games timely and make it a condition for a player to be a starter.

Always remember to look after the safety of your players.

WARM-UP ON GAME DAY

The day of the game can be an exciting time. Players, coaches, parents, and spectators get excited. Irrespective of the situation, always bring your players to warm up for the game. You should know the warm-ups that get your players juiced up and ready for the game.

Commonly, youth football teams warm up by following the specialist, SAQ, individual, and team periods. SAQ is an abbreviation for speed, agility, and quickness. This warm-up process starts with preparing quarterbacks and special teams kicking, throwing, and catching the ball. The wide receivers work on their primary running routes.

Ensure that you start slowly and progress to more intense warm-ups. After the specialist period, the following are the whole team dynamic warm-ups. Finally, run drills for your offense, defense, and special teams. Remember to keep these periods short, as your aim is to prepare players for the game.

THE GAME PLAN

You should have a written game plan just as you've had written practice plans. No game plan means you might win games by chance. The problem is that winning this way is unpredictable and will need to be clarified for your young players.

Write all the plays you'll employ in offense, defense, and special teams in your game plan. Include your best running, passing, and defensive plays in your plan. You should know what your team will do on the first down, second down, and third down. Are you going to punt or run the ball on fourth down? How are you going to defend on your goal line? Make your plan as comprehensive as possible.

Your game plan is only complete with a substitution plan or a plan on alternating players. There must be an integration between the plays you'll execute at different phases of the game and alternating players.

Remember that your game plan starts shaping when you scout the opponent's defense, offense, and special teams.

IN-GAME COACHING

During the game, you'll have to bark a lot of instructions from the sidelines, including play calling. Your players will need a lot of reminding throughout the game. One of the critical decisions you'll need to make for successful in-game coaching is who starts and who begins on the substitution bench. Like I've said multiple times, knowing your roster is crucial.

Based on the league rules, consider playing everyone for some portion of the game. This means you need a substitution strategy that can give you an advantage when it matters most. You can implement two substitution strategies: substituting individually or substituting by quarters.

Substituting individually: Occurs when you replace one player for another. It's the best method of getting the most competitive combination of players during the game. Although it makes it hard to track playtime, you can assign this task to a parent or assistant coach. This also makes it crucial to know the number of plays per player that the league rules allow. You can also substitute players by series of plays when using this strategy.

Substituting by quarters: This technique means you substitute players after each quarter. It's easy to track the playing time for each player.

Statistics are crucial because they help you avoid bias. Generally, you should keep statistics of your plays during the game. You can use these figures to review and decide on the best plays after each drive.

IN-GAME ADJUSTMENTS

It's rare to significantly adjust your team tactics during a game, especially at the 8–9 and 10–11 age levels. Still, in-game adjustments are necessary to exploit the opponent's weaknesses. Adjustments you could make include the timing of substitutions to execute certain plays. The basis of in-game adjustments should be a thorough analysis of the opponent. Here are some pointers to guide you when adjusting:

- Check how and adjust to how your opponent's run the ball.
- Look and adapt to how the quarterback throws when under pressure.
- Check if the linebackers need to be faster on running back sweep plays.
- Assess if the defensive backs are less skilled or slow.

Adjustments based on your opponent's tendencies can result in your team winning. Remember to simplify your in-game adjustment without taking out the fun of playing the game for the children.

CORRECTING IN-GAME MISTAKES

There's no doubt that children will make mistakes during the game. How you react can make or break a child or the team. Errors will be made by individuals, the team, or both. It's during such situations that your coaching will be tested.

The truth is that you'll need to do something about those mistakes. Many of us learn a ton from our mistakes. The adjustments make us better, which is the same for your players. You should take these two actions to handle mistakes.

Give your players a cooling-off period: Acting immediately after a mistake can trigger an emotional burst in a child. They can feel inadequate and not be ready to deal with it at that time. This is not unique to children, as it happens with adults. After a mistake, encourage your players to keep going. Wait until the next training day to discuss the mistake with your team or individual player. It's best to discuss individual mistakes with the concerned player only.

Focus more on the positives: We all feel good when people talk positively about us. The same goes for youth football players. When discussing mistakes, first focus on the sound plays, decisions, and tackles the player made. When they're in a receptive frame of mind, help them see how minimizing the mistake you saw could make them and the team better.

COACHING CONDUCT

Your conduct during the game influences the behavior of your players. If you curse or yell at the referee, opposite coach, or assistant coach, your players, and their parents will likely follow suit. Whatever your emotion —anxious or down, enthusiastic or overly angry—your team will reflect it on the field.

I've discussed the importance of having a parents' meeting before the start of the season. One of the critical qualities I stated is that you should lead by example. This means you should follow the behavior guidelines you expect from your parents and players.

Youth football, although you want to win games, is about developing great people while having fun. That's why you should be as positive as you can throughout the game. You want to talk with your players and others in this state of mind. Staying calm under pressure is the mark of having self-control.

PLAYER CONDUCT

It's your job to maintain control of your team during the game. If you lead by example and respect the opponents, your players will likely copy that behavior. They will also probably copy negative behavior if that's how you act.

Your team's rule should be that you will not tolerate bad behavior. It's a good idea to make this rule a condition for a player to start or stay on the football field during a game. You should follow up on a player's bad behavior with a one-on-one talk in the manner described earlier.

HALFTIME

Many actions I discussed earlier apply during halftime. You should see halftime as a time to pump up and enthuse your players. It's worthwhile doing this after you've discussed with the players and assistant coaches what adjustments will be made.

While having these discussions, provide players with fruits such as oranges or bananas to replenish nutrients and energy sources. It's a good idea to also offer Gatorade. After the halftime team talk, get your players to stretch to prepare for kickoff.

AFTER THE GAME

Unless a football is washed out or postponed for some reason, there'll always be a result: a win, loss, or tie. As much as it's essential to winning, it does nothing if you don't welcome other kinds of results. Sportsmanship is still important whether the game ends in defeat, win, or tie. Always shake hands with the opponents at the end of each game.

I know winning can bring out emotions, and players and coaches might misbehave. Winning doesn't mean you have to belittle the opponents because they probably gave their best to win. Your team was too good for them on the day.

Sportsmanship is about working together to develop excellent human beings, not just great players. Taunting your opponents doesn't add any positive things to the opponent's players. If anything, it can create negativity, and some children might even stop playing the game, which is not good.

Remember to check the health condition of injured players, if any. Always ensure that every player is safe after the game and that parents are available to collect each one.

POST-GAME TEAM CIRCLE

Make it a rule that players should take a knee after each game. Ensure you chat with the coaches about what to say during the post-game meeting. Have one of the coaches address them: praising them on what they did well and reinforcing the desire of the team to keep improving.

It's also a good time to reward performance with team-building fun activities and juicy slices of pizza. Make sure to stay after the fun activities to ensure that every player has left for home.

10

WHAT TO DO AT THE END OF THE SEASON

The season was long and tough. It took a lot out of the players, coaches, parents, and supporters. Whether you've won the National Championships or only a few games, your team deserves a celebration. This is the time to celebrate the time spent by players, coaches, parents, and every stakeholder for their effort in building children up and a youth football team. What should you do at the end of the season?

The first thing is to celebrate and then get together with the coaches to review and prepare for the next season. In this chapter, I've divided the actions to take into these two categories of what you need to do.

WHAT TO DO TO CELEBRATE YOUR TEAM'S END OF THE SEASON

Sometimes it can be hard to have everyone at your end-of-the-season celebration party. If this isn't a concern, you can set a date and location for these celebrations. On the other hand, it's much easier to have everyone present if you celebrate your team's end of the season after the league's final game.

Whether you hold the party after your last season game or at a particular date and location, there are some actions to take to leave lasting memories.

Have a Team Banquet

It's a good idea to have a team banquet if celebrating soon after the last game of the season doesn't interest you. This can be in the form of a cookout or team potluck. The final decisions will lie with the team organizing the event.

Although food and decor are important, what's most crucial is what gets done to celebrate the occasion. One of the key activities you'll do will be to award trophies and certificates to players and other recipients. No child should feel like they didn't win anything, so it's best to dish out awards for various categories. For example, you can hand out a certificate to each player who participated on your team during the season. A small trophy inscribed with the child's name would be a better award. You, your assistant coaches, and other staff members will decide on the best method to award all the players.

It's a great idea to record the event and take photos of the team, players, and other attendees.

Consider unique awards to ensure you promote the ultimate aim of youth football: to develop great players and individuals. Here are some ideas for special awards:

Good sportsmanship: Recognize your players for demonstrating good sportsmanship throughout the season. You can bring in the players and parents to vote for deserving players.

Exceptional statistics: During the season, you will have outstanding players on offense, defense, and special teams. Awarding players in these different roles allows many of your players to shine.

Good Attitudes: Optimism is a great attitude for a great person. Since youth football is about developing players and wonderful people, why not have an award for a player who demonstrated an excellent attitude throughout the season? For example, you can be awarded "The Most Likely Player to Coach Teammates" or "The Most Resilient Player."

Let this be a mind-jogger for the awards you can hand out at your end-of-season team banquet.

Remember to appreciate parents, volunteers, and sponsors. Running a youth football team (or any other team) requires resources—tangible and intangible. Parents, volunteers, and sponsors chip in with various resources to help the team succeed. They, therefore, deserve appreciation at your team banquet. Perhaps you might have one or two awards for these people.

The same can be said about the spouses of the coaches. It takes time and effort to coach youngsters. Coaches must invest much effort and time in developing youth football players. Spouses remain with a lot more to do at home than usual. They deserve to be thanked for their actions and help build your team.

One of the important items during the celebration is a speech by someone playing at higher levels of football. It should be a person who started at the bottom and progressed through the ranks to reach those higher levels. It doesn't have to be an NFL player since a college player would be fine. Ask them to emphasize the importance of discipline on and off the field; the respect of parents, coaches, teammates, and opponents; and the value of hard work.

Hold Coach Meetings

The second important activity at the end of the season is coach meetings. These are meetings where you review the season that has just ended, plan for the upcoming season, and lay the foundation for the program's future.

Each coach meeting should have a purpose and an agenda to focus the discussion around that objective. A meeting must have a direction to produce desired results. Besides the agenda, each coaching meeting should be attended by the head coach, assistant coaches, and any member of staff involved in running the youth football program. Even if a coaching staff member isn't available next season, include them because they'll add value based on their involvement in the previous season.

The items you should add to the agenda include evaluating player performance; practices; schemes you used; the effectiveness of offense, defense, and special teams; and assessing the team's results. After all these evaluations, coaches should set expectations for the next season.

It's easy to fall into the trap of trying to evaluate every player on the team. You'll likely need more time for this. Instead, select a couple of players, say 10–15, and evaluate each. For each player, check if they understood their role in the team, played as expected, played out of position, and how they played in big moments. Whatever issues you find, you'll know what to address in the coming season.

Remember that as you evaluate players, you will likely find that you, as coaches, made mistakes. It's important to acknowledge those mistakes and work out a plan to address them.

Watching videos of your team's past season games is best for the coach meetings to be effective. As the head coach, ensure that you hand out templates to your assistant coaches to record information to evaluate players. I suggest creating templates for each phase of football so that an assistant coach can be more focused.

One area of a youth football game to check how you perform is situational football. I'm talking about two-minute offense and two-minute defense. Many coaches should spend more time on situational football. You might be surprised to learn that you lost a couple of games because you handled clock management poorly. Whatever your findings, the feedback will be necessary for planning the following season.

CONCLUSION

You now have learned a ton about coaching youth football. To help you keep your learning fresh, here's a quick summary of the main points covered throughout this book.

Chapter 1 introduced you to the qualities of elite youth coaches. To be an elite coach, lead by example, and demonstrate integrity, discipline, resilience, hard work, and organization. Developing great players is easier if you communicate effectively, create and maintain healthy competition, and keep practices upbeat. Best of all, lead by example so children can learn good attitudes and habits from you.

Chapter 2 took you through how to choose assistant coaches. Qualities to look for include respect and loyalty, in addition to the qualities exhibited by elite coaches. You can find good assistant coaches. They may be available within your circle. For example, one of the parents or a former teammate from high school. Remember to conduct a preseason parent meeting for practices and games to proceed as planned.

In Chapter 3, you learned about the fundamentals of football, including positions and their roles. Some key positions include quarterback, kicker, center, and defensive line players. It's essential to understand each player's role to use them appropriately. You were introduced to how the three-point stance works.

Armed with the fundamentals, you were introduced to the power of having a written practice plan. Two things to remember are scouting your opponents and evaluating the performance of your players weekly. For example, it makes it easier for players, assistant coaches, and parents to follow your lead. All these were covered in Chapter 4.

Chapter 5 dealt with offensive, defensive, and special teams drills. These are important because they teach your players the right way to play football. The skills learned in Chapter 5 are the basis of how you coach offense, defense, and special teams, as covered in Chapters 6, 7, and 8. The key to winning games is performing drills, whether coaching offense, defense, or special teams. Be patient and drill your players on the fundamentals.

Chapter 9 focused on the implementation of techniques you taught in Chapters 5, 6, 7, and 8 during the game. Ensure that you and your players respect the opponents all the time. Your play-calling strategies at different stages will win you games. Remember to warm up players before they start playing for their health. Approach each game with a plan based on your scouting of the opponents. Be sure to call plays that your players practiced.

When the season ends, celebrate it with parents, children, and your staff. During the celebrations, give awards to deserving players, parents, and anyone who played a significant role during the season. Ensure that all the players get recognition to keep them pumped up and interested in the football game.

Let me remind you about the ultimate goal of coaching youth football:

"Winning games is the low-hanging fruit of your football program; helping your players learn the techniques and principles of football, as well as becoming physically fit and molding good sportsmanship in football and life, are the ultimate long-term goals! Your young athletes are 'winning' when becoming better human beings through their participation in football. Keep that perspective in mind when you coach. It is a privilege to set the tone for how your team approaches the game. Continue to win in all aspects of competition in proper perspective, and your young children will follow your lead."

If this book had taught you one or more practical actions to take when coaching youth football, it would have done its job. Someone out there may be looking for such actionable guidance, and this book could be valuable to them. Why not leave a glowing review on Amazon so that such people can find it? Most importantly, go ahead and implement the ideas I've shared with you right away!

GLOSSARY

Blitz: When five or more defensive players rush through the line of scrimmage to thwart the offensive team's attack. The aim is often to run into the backfield to try to 'sack' the quarterback.

Blocking: A technique in which offensive players use their bodies and arms to block defenders from making tackles. This moves them away from the path of the ball carrier.

Bomb: An above-average forward pass.

Buttonhook: A pass route in which a wide receiver runs a certain distance straight ahead several yards before suddenly turning back to catch the pass.

Dead ball: A situation in which the ball is no longer in play such as when the down officially ends. Other dead ball situations include when the official declares the end of live ball.

Down: A play from the snap of the ball at the line of scrimmage until the player in possession of the ball goes out of bounds, is tackled, spikes the ball, or takes a knee.

Drive: A series of plays when the offense possesses the ball are advancing toward the goal.

Extra point: Immediately following a touchdown, a team gets an opportunity to add another field goal from the opponent's two-yard line by kicking the ball between the uprights of the goal posts.

Fair catch: A situation when, on a punted ball, the punt receiver waves their hand in the air to indicate that they won't advance the play. The opposing team players don't tackle such a punt receiver.

Field goal: A play that's worth three points if the ball goes between the uprights and crossbar of the opponent's goal post. It's often used when the offensive team is close to the opponent's goal posts or on any other down when play time is running out.

Forward pass: A play in which the offensive team throws the ball from behind the line of scrimmage. For the pass to be complete, the ball must be caught. A forward pass is permitted if the ball hasn't crossed the line of scrimmage.

Fumble: A situation in which the ball carrier drops the ball in the field. The team that recovers first gains possession of the ball. If the defending team gains possession, the fumble becomes a turnover.

Grounding: A situation in which an offensive quarterback throws the ball down on the field to avoid a blitz.

Hand off: A play in which an offensive player hands the ball to a teammate.

Huddle: The gathering of players in a circle before each down to discuss the next and the quarterback often leads those discussions.

Interception: When a defender catches a forward pass, resulting in a turnover.

Kicker: An offensive player tasked with kicking the ball during attempts of scoring extra points, kickoffs, and field goals.

Kickoff: A play that occurs at the start of each half and after each score when a player kicks the ball to the defending team.

Lateral: Also called a backward pass, it's a pass that occurs when a player who's ahead of the line of scrimmage throws the ball to a teammate beside or behind them, but not in front of them.

Line of scrimmage: It's an imaginary parallel to the goal lines and both teams set up across it on each down. It's mandatory for the offensive team to have a minimum of seven players on or within a foot of it.

Neutral zone: A zone that covers an area of one yard that encompasses the line of scrimmage and separates the offense and defense teams.

Onside kick: A kickoff attempt in which a team tries to regain possession of the ball. The offensive team kicks the ball a short distance forward to allow its players to compete and recover the ball. It's a must that the kicked ball must travel a minimum of ten yards before the offense team's players can recover the ball.

Pass rush: A play by the defensive team to rush the quarterback of the offensive team by tackling them before they pass the ball.

Place kick: A play used at the start of each half, on field goals, on extra points attempts, and after every score in which the kicker player places the ball on the ground and a teammate holds it before they kick it. The ball may also be placed on a kicking tee for the kicker.

Punt: A play in which the kicker behind the line of scrimmage drops the ball from their hands and punts it before it touches the ground. Teams often punts the ball on the fourth down after they've had three failed first three downs.

Rushing: The act of using running plays to move the ball forward while on offense.

Sack: A defensive play resulting in tackling the offensive team's quarterback behind the line of scrimmage to deny the offense again in yards.

Safety: A play that results in two points to the defense team when the offense team fumbles the ball out of their end zone, commits a foul in their end zone, or is tackled within their end zone.

Screen pass: A short forward pass in which the quarterback fakes a long pass but throws the ball to a receiver behind the rushing defense.

Shotgun: A play in which the quarterback stands several yards behind the center to catch the snap and have more than usual time to throw the ball.

Snap: Tossing of the ball by the center through their legs to the place kick holder, quarterback, or punter.

Spot: A location in the field where the ball is placed after each play to position the line of scrimmage.

Sweep: A rushing outside play in which the quarterback hands the ball to the running back who runs parallel to the line of scrimmage instead of through the middle of the offensive line.

Tackle: A play in which the defense player takes down or stops the ball carrier.

Touch back: A kickoff play in which the defense catches the ball in the end zone and doesn't run it out or the ball goes through the end zone. The defense player who catches the ball kneels on one knee in the end zone to signal a touch back. To begin the next offensive play, the ball gets played from the twenty-yard line.

Touchdown: A play that's worth six points that occurs when a player ball carrier crosses the opposing goal line or recovers or catches the ball in the opposing team's end zone.

Turnover: A play that results from an interception or fumble by the offense leading to the defense team gaining possession of the ball.

REFERENCES

Clear, J. (n.d.). *Vince Lombardi on the hidden power of mastering the fundamentals*. James Clear. https://jamesclear.com/vince-lombardi-fundamentals

Impelman, C. (2017, October 4). *What it means to be a person of integrity*. Coach John Wooden. https://www.thewoodeneffect.com/integrity/

Matava, M. J. (2019, March). *Football injuries in young athletes*. Ortho-Info. https://orthoinfo.aaos.org/en/staying-healthy/ortho-pinion-football-injuries-in-young-athletes

Online Etymology Dictionary. (2021, October 13). *integrity | Origin and meaning of integrity by Online Etymology Dictionary*. Online Etymology Dictionary. https://www.etymonline.com/word/integrity

Project Play. (n.d.). *Youth sports facts: Benefits*. The Aspen Institute Project Play. https://www.aspenprojectplay.org/youth-sports/facts/benefits

Purcell, L. K. (2013). Sport nutrition for young athletes. *Pediatrics & Child Health, 18*(4), 200–205. https://doi.org/10.1093/pch/18.4.200

Ryan, J. (2014, October 21). *Examining luck in NFL turnovers*. The Harvard Sports Analysis Collective. https://harvardsportsanalysis.org/2014/10/how-random-are-turnovers/